Police Brutality

Other Books in the Current Controversies Series:

The Abortion Controversy
Alcoholism
Assisted Suicide
Computers and Society
Conserving the Environment
Crime
The Disabled
Drug Trafficking
Ethics
Europe
Family Violence
Free Speech
Gambling
Garbage and Waste
Gay Rights
Genetics and Intelligence
Gun Control
Hate Crimes
Hunger
Illegal Drugs
Illegal Immigration

The Information Highway
Interventionism
Iraq
Marriage and Divorce
Mental Health
Minorities
Nationalism and Ethnic
    Conflict
Native American Rights
Politicians and Ethics
Pollution
Racism
Reproductive Technologies
Sexual Harassment
Smoking
Teen Addiction
Urban Terrorism
Violence Against Women
Violence in the Media
Women in the Military

Police Brutality

Tamara L. Roleff, *Book Editor*

David Bender, *Publisher*
Bruno Leone, *Executive Editor*

Bonnie Szumski, *Editorial Director*
Brenda Stalcup, *Managing Editor*
Scott Barbour, *Senior Editor*

CURRENT CONTROVERSIES

Cover photo: © Frances M. Roberts

Library of Congress Cataloging-in-Publication Data

Police brutality / Tamara L. Roleff, book editor.
    p. cm. — (Current controversies)
    Includes bibliographical references and index.
    ISBN 0-7377-0013-0 (lib. : alk. paper). — ISBN 0-7377-0012-2
(pbk. : alk. paper)
    1. Police brutality—United States. I. Roleff, Tamara L., 1959–   .
II. Series.
HV8141.P564   1999
363.2'32—dc21   98-26633
                                           CIP

©1999 by Greenhaven Press, Inc., PO Box 289009, San Diego, CA 92198-9009
Printed in the U.S.A.

Contents

Foreword   10

Introduction   12

Chapter 1: Is Police Brutality a Serious Problem?

Chapter Preface   16

Yes: Police Brutality Is a Serious Problem

Police Brutality Is a Serious Problem *by Amnesty International*   17
A decade-long survey of cases of police ill-treatment and use of excessive
force reveals that police brutality is a serious problem in New York City.
Claims against the city have been increasing for many years, as has the
number of damage awards the city has paid to injured people. In addition,
the number of civilians who have died in police custody and from police
shootings has also risen. The extent of police brutality cannot be determined by counting the number of lawsuits filed against the city because
many cases do not result in lawsuits.

Brutality by Federal Law Enforcement Agents Is a Serious Problem
by Catherine M. Farmer   21
A pattern of paramilitary assaults on innocent civilians by federal law enforcement is well documented. The powers and number of federal police
have outstripped those specified by the U.S. Constitution. The size and
power of federal law enforcement must be curtailed.

Police Brutality Against Minorities Is a Serious Problem
by Bernice Powell Jackson   24
Minorities across the nation are the targets of police brutality and harassment. Not only are minorities harassed because of the color of their skin,
but they are also subject to injustice in the legal system.

Police Brutality Against Hispanics Is a Serious Problem
by Michael Huspek   26
Complaints of brutality against law officers in the Immigration and Naturalization Service (INS) increased dramatically in the mid-1990s. Since
nearly all the complaints against the INS in the southwestern United
States are lodged by Hispanics, it is evident that Latinos are targeted by
the INS and are the victims of discrimination.

Brutality Against Prisoners Is a Serious Problem
by Ben Chaney and Karen Carrillo   30
The criminal justice system in Mississippi jails and prisons is out of

control. Too many black prisoners are dying while in police custody. The official explanations of accidental death or suicide are suspect. The only way to end questionable prisoner deaths is through constant exposure of police brutality and abuse.

The Media Downplay Police Brutality *by* Revolutionary Worker   36
Police brutality is criminal behavior and must not be tolerated. Instead of documenting how people cope when a family member has been brutalized or killed by the police, the major news media whitewash police behavior. The only way to achieve justice for victims of police brutality is to get the true story out to the public.

No: Police Brutality Is Not a Serious Problem

The Extent of Police Brutality Is Exaggerated *by William J. Bratton*   39
An August 1997 incident of police brutality in New York City has led to charges that such mistreatment is pervasive. However, one incident of police brutality should not result in the condemnation of an entire police department that is doing a good job of reducing the crime rate. As the number of police officers increases, so too will the number of brutality complaints because more of the public will come in contact with the police. The number of complaints will decrease as rookie police officers learn how to interact with the public without offending or fighting with people.

The Use of Extreme Force Is Sometimes Justified
by Sarah J. McCarthy   41
All instances of police brutality are tragic, but there are times when police need to use excessive force to protect themselves or the lives of others. Blacks who accuse the police of brutality should instead accept responsibility for their criminal acts.

Brutality Against Illegal Immigrants Is Exaggerated *by John Corry*   44
Illegal immigrants who break the law and endanger the lives of others should not expect to be treated gently when they are arrested, nor should they be allowed to sue the police for their injuries. On the whole, the United States treats its illegal immigrants better than other countries do.

Efforts to Reduce Police Brutality Should Not Interfere with
Effective Crime Control *by George L. Kelling*   48
The police have played an important role in reducing the crime rate in cities across the United States. Order was returned to the streets as police moved out of their cars and started walking their beats again. While police brutality is deplorable, efforts to reduce it must not interfere with the police's function of controlling crime.

Media Reports of Police Brutality Are Incomplete *by Nancy L. Ford*   52
A videotaped episode of a police beating misleads the public. The heavily edited version of the videotape does not include all the events that happened prior to the beating. It is unfair to the police to judge them without knowing all the facts of the case.

The Media Overemphasize Police Brutality *by Joseph Sobran*   55
A police brutality case in New York City received extensive media coverage only because it was so horrific. Many violent crimes—including murders—receive much less coverage, if any at all, because they are less

graphically disturbing or racially tinged. The media slant the news by selectively reporting some facts but not others.

Chapter 2: What Factors Contribute to Police Brutality?

Chapter Preface   58

Racism Causes Police Brutality *by Salim Muwakkil*   59
Racism has been and continues to be pervasive throughout police forces across the country. When police officers act on their racist assumptions, it is frequently poor black people who are their victims. New technology now permits the public to witness this racism in action.

Police Often Overreact to Challenges to Their Authority
by Deborah Sontag and Dan Barry   64
Many police perceive a challenge to their authority as not merely disrespectful, but a threat to their safety and the balance of power. In order to maintain their power over civilians, some police may attempt to dominate them through physical force, which may lead to the use of excessive force.

Assertive Policing Contributes to Police Brutality *by Dennis Cauchon*   72
Assertive policing is an aggressive tactic that targets minor offenses such as jaywalking and disturbing the peace in the hopes of deterring more serious crime. Assertive policing has been credited for reducing crime rates in many cities. However, an increased number of police brutality charges seem to be an inevitable result of assertive policing as more civilians come in contact with police.

Police Attitudes Contribute to Police Brutality
by Jerome H. Skolnick and James J. Fyfe   76
Police officers see themselves as the "thin blue line" that separates criminals from the rest of society. To them, policing is not just a job, but a way of life. Some officers feel threatened when their authority is defied and may attempt to regain control through physical domination of the civilian.

Police Culture Causes Police Brutality *by* Chicago Citizen   80
Many people become police officers because they want to exercise authority and control over others. Police officers are trained to see the public, especially blacks, as the enemy who must be controlled. Police loyalty and fraternity protect those officers who commit acts of brutality from prosecution, thus allowing them to brutalize again.

Chapter 3: How Does Police Brutality Affect Society?

Chapter Preface   83

Police Brutality Reveals the Injustice of Capitalism *by George Kane*   84
Police are given the right to use violence as a means of enforcing social order and protecting the power and property of capitalists. The police do not use their power to defend the working classes, but to punish them. Police abuse is so widely acknowledged that society has lost its respect for the police's power and authority. This respect is essential if the police are to enforce the will of the capitalists.

Police Brutality Reveals Society's Racism *by Joseph C. Kennedy*   89
Black men are the frequent targets of police brutality and abuse. Harassing
and brutalizing blacks because of the color of their skin reveals a racism
that runs deep in the heart of police culture as well as society at large.

Police Brutality Leads to a Loss of Trust in the Police
by Lawrence J. Finnegan Jr.   98
The tendency of police officers to protect each other against charges of
brutality only causes the public to distrust the police and the official investigation into the charges. Even good officers become less trustworthy
in the public's eyes as the belief that the police are abusive and corrupt
gains acceptance. The only way to earn back the public's trust is to ap-
point an independent review board to monitor police behavior.

Police Brutality Results in a Loss of Respect for the Police
by Washington Afro-American   101
Each incident of brutality causes people to lose respect for the police.
Physical abuse only causes people to think of the police as the enemy.
Respect can only be earned by giving respect.

Police Brutality Makes Citizens Feel Less Safe
by Dianne Liuzzi Hagan   104
People who constantly fear that they or their loved ones will be harassed
or brutalized by the police because of their skin color do not feel safe.
People can only begin to feel safe when the police learn that such behavior will not be tolerated.

Chapter 4: How Can Police Brutality Be Reduced?

Preventing Police Brutality: An Overview *by Richard Lacayo*   108
An increasing number of cities have realized that police brutality is a serious problem. They have established various procedures to identify, discipline, and retrain abusive police officers as well as to investigate complaints of police brutality. Policing strategies and their effects on these
communities have also come under review.

Radical Changes Are Needed to Counter Police Brutality
by People Against Racist Terror   112
Police brutality is a relentless and systematic problem in American society because the role of the police is to act as an occupying army in oppressed communities and as border guards for wealthy areas. Any solution proposed to deal with police brutality must include multiple actions,
the most important of which is community control of the police.

The Police Must Be Subject to Community Oversight
by American Civil Liberties Union   117
Community oversight of police forces can reduce the incidence of police
brutality. Complaints about police brutality should be investigated by a
civilian review board. Communities should develop policies concerning
police shootings and the use of force. Furthermore, all police policies
must be subject to public review.

Civilian Review Boards Must Police the Police *by Lynne Wilson*   124
Law enforcement agencies are vehemently opposed to giving civilian re-

view boards oversight of police brutality complaints. The agencies believe they are capable of policing their own members without outside interference. However, law enforcement agencies that rely on internal affairs procedures to investigate and discipline officers accused of police brutality are more concerned with defending the officers involved than protecting the public interest. Despite the intense opposition from police departments, civilian review boards are essential to curb police brutality, corruption, and racism.

The Police Must Be Involved in Their Communities
by *National Association for the Advancement of Colored People*   133
Many police officers believe that the citizens in their community are the enemy. To combat that perception, police officers should live in or near the area they patrol; participate in community activities; be accountable to the community for their actions; and be representative of the community they serve.

Public Officials Must Denounce Police Brutality by *David N. Dinkins*   140
The integrity of an organization is determined by its leaders. The police commissioner and the mayor must take responsibility for their police department by speaking out against and punishing instances of police brutality. Their silence implies that police brutality is tolerated and acceptable.

The Police Must Be Held Accountable for Their Actions
by *John DeSantis*   148
Police brutality is pervasive in America, but its presence is denied or excused by many people, including some of the highest community leaders. Society allows the police to unlawfully brutalize citizens because many of the victims are perceived to be deserving of the abuse. The only way to stop police brutality is to demand that the police are held accountable for their actions.

Congressional Oversight of Federal Law Enforcement Agencies
Would Reduce Brutality by *Robert J. Caldwell*   154
Federal law enforcement agents have brutalized and killed many innocent civilians. Those in charge of the federal agencies have not taken responsibility for their agents' misconduct. Therefore, it is up to Congress to demand that those responsible for such brutality be held accountable.

Communities Must Stand Up to the Police by *Van Jones*   158
More and more residents are rebelling against police who brutalize their innocent neighbors. If this rage against the police can be channeled into strategic campaigns to fight for police reform, sweeping changes can be made to improve society.

Bibliography   160
Organizations to Contact   163
Index   166

Foreword

By definition, controversies are "discussions of questions in which opposing opinions clash" (Webster's Twentieth Century Dictionary Unabridged). Few would deny that controversies are a pervasive part of the human condition and exist on virtually every level of human enterprise. Controversies transpire between individuals and among groups, within nations and between nations. Controversies supply the grist necessary for progress by providing challenges and challengers to the status quo. They also create atmospheres where strife and warfare can flourish. A world without controversies would be a peaceful world; but it also would be, by and large, static and prosaic.

The Series' Purpose

The purpose of the Current Controversies series is to explore many of the social, political, and economic controversies dominating the national and international scenes today. Titles selected for inclusion in the series are highly focused and specific. For example, from the larger category of criminal justice, Current Controversies deals with specific topics such as police brutality, gun control, white collar crime, and others. The debates in Current Controversies also are presented in a useful, timeless fashion. Articles and book excerpts included in each title are selected if they contribute valuable, long-range ideas to the overall debate. And wherever possible, current information is enhanced with historical documents and other relevant materials. Thus, while individual titles are current in focus, every effort is made to ensure that they will not become quickly outdated. Books in the Current Controversies series will remain important resources for librarians, teachers, and students for many years.

In addition to keeping the titles focused and specific, great care is taken in the editorial format of each book in the series. Book introductions and chapter prefaces are offered to provide background material for readers. Chapters are organized around several key questions that are answered with diverse opinions representing all points on the political spectrum. Materials in each chapter include opinions in which authors clearly disagree as well as alternative opinions in which authors may agree on a broader issue but disagree on the possible solutions. In this way, the content of each volume in Current Controversies mirrors the mosaic of opinions encountered in society. Readers will quickly realize that there are many viable answers to these complex issues. By questioning each author's conclusions, students and casual readers can begin to develop the critical thinking skills so important to evaluating opinionated material.

Current Controversies is also ideal for controlled research. Each anthology in the series is composed of primary sources taken from a wide gamut of informational categories including periodicals, newspapers, books, United States and foreign government documents, and the publications of private and public organizations. Readers will find factual support for reports, debates, and research papers covering all areas of important issues. In addition, an annotated table of contents, an index, a book and periodical bibliography, and a list of organizations to contact are included in each book to expedite further research.

Perhaps more than ever before in history, people are confronted with diverse and contradictory information. During the Persian Gulf War, for example, the public was not only treated to minute-to-minute coverage of the war, it was also inundated with critiques of the coverage and countless analyses of the factors motivating U.S. involvement. Being able to sort through the plethora of opinions accompanying today's major issues, and to draw one's own conclusions, can be a complicated and frustrating struggle. It is the editors' hope that Current Controversies will help readers with this struggle.

> *"Just as in 1991, Americans in 1997 were confronted with images of extreme police violence against a black man, causing them to wonder if such cases were aberrations or typical of the treatment minorities receive from police officers."*

Introduction

Early in the morning on August 9, 1997, police officers from the 70th precinct in Brooklyn, New York, were called to quell a disturbance at a nightclub in East Flatbush. Abner Louima, a Haitian immigrant, was leaving the nightclub with relatives when the police officers arrived. During the melee that ensued, a black man punched a white officer, Justin Volpe, in the face. The slugger escaped, so, according to witnesses, the enraged Volpe grabbed Louima, the first black man he saw. Louima was arrested, handcuffed, and put into the back seat of a patrol car driven by officers Thomas Wiese and Charles Schwarz. Louima claims that while on the way to the police station, the officers—joined by Volpe and his partner Thomas Bruder—stopped the car twice to beat him with their police radios and nightsticks, all the while cursing him and shouting racial slurs at him.

Once at the police station, Louima was charged with second-degree assault, disorderly conduct, and resisting arrest. He contends that the officers strip-searched him and forced him to walk handcuffed to a bathroom with his pants around his ankles in full view of everyone in the station. In the bathroom, Louima claims, Schwarz held him down while Volpe shoved the handle of a toilet plunger up his rectum while yelling that this would teach him to respect a cop. Then, Louima maintains, Volpe rammed the handle into his mouth, breaking several of his teeth in the process. After the assault, Louima asked to be taken to a hospital, but the paramedics were not allowed to take him for an hour and a half. At the hospital, doctors determined that he had sustained serious injuries, including a ruptured spleen, punctured bladder, and a hole in his intestinal wall.

The *New York Daily News* broke the story of Louima's beating four days later after a columnist received a phone tip from an anonymous 70th precinct police officer. The subsequent stories and columns caused a huge outcry against police brutality not only in New York City but across the nation as well. All charges against Louima were dropped. Volpe and Schwarz were immediately suspended and indicted for aggravated sexual assault and first-degree assault. A week later, Wiese and Bruder were arrested and charged with second- and third-degree assault and criminal possession of a weapon—the police radio that they reportedly used to beat Louima. A fifth officer, Michael Bellomo, was also charged with attempting to cover up the beating.

The outcry following the Louima case was reminiscent of the response to the 1991 beating of black motorist Rodney King by white police officers in Los Angeles. Much of King's beating was videotaped by an unobserved bystander. The videotape was broadcast nationwide and sparked a national uproar over police brutality. Four of the officers involved in the beating were tried and acquitted of police brutality charges by an all-white jury in 1992. More than fifty people were killed during several days of rioting that followed the trial. Just as in 1991, Americans in 1997 were confronted with images of extreme police violence against a black man, causing them to wonder if such cases were aberrations or typical of the treatment minorities receive from police officers. City and police officials across the country insist that cases of police brutality such as the King and Louima beatings are isolated incidents. According to New York City mayor Rudolph Giuliani and police commissioner Howard Safir, the police officers involved in the Louima case are merely a couple of "bad apples" who are spoiling the reputation of the country's finest police department. "The overwhelming majority of police officers are good people doing a good job," Giuliani maintains. Safir adds, "This police commissioner and this mayor, I know, will tolerate no racism, no abuse, and no undue force or unprofessionalism by any police officer and we're not going to tolerate it in this case." Most importantly, Safir asserts, such a case of police brutality is an uncommon police experience. "Although [the Louima case is] a horrific event, it's a rare event," he contends. It is much more typical, he argues, for a police officer to be killed in the line of duty than for an officer to brutalize an innocent civilian.

Law enforcement and other public officials maintain that the media exaggerate the extent and severity of alleged police brutality. Emphasizing incidents such as the Louima and King beatings distorts the true nature of police work, which is to prevent crime and help people, they contend. Moreover, although many of the brutality complaints against police officers are filed by blacks and other minorities, supporters of the police assert that it is unfair to label police officers as racist. Minorities represent a higher proportion of their arrests and brutality cases because police officers are most likely to be working in high-crime neighborhoods where the inhabitants are mostly poor or black, they explain. Jon DeSantis, author of *The New Untouchables*, writes that "police violence becomes a mere symptom of the underlying problems" of racism and that the police should not be blamed for the existence of those problems.

Many civil rights groups contend, however, that incidents such as the Louima and King beatings are not isolated cases of police brutality. They believe that these beatings are indicative of a pervasive attitude found throughout police departments across the country in which the officers assume that such actions are condoned and tolerated. The attack against Louima, according to Brooklyn district attorney Charles Hynes, was "an act of almost incomprehensible depravity" that was committed "with the apparent expectation that they would get away with it." Critics claim that police officers are practically immune from any charges of police brutality brought against them. For example, a study by the New York Civil Liberties Union found that the Civilian Complaint Review Board (CCRB), which reviews charges of police brutality in the city, substantiated only 4.3 percent of the 16,327 cases of brutality brought before the board between 1993 and 1996. Only 1 percent of the officers involved in the substantiated cases were disciplined. The most severe punishment the officers received, the study noted, was the loss of ten to fifteen days of vacation. Another study cited by critics found that of the 133 charges of police brutality filed in July 1997, police supervisors threw out, dropped, or cleared 70 percent of the cases before they even reached the review board.

Lawyers and civil rights groups also note that complaints about police abuse have increased dramatically across the country since the Abner Louima case was first publicized. In New York City, the CCRB used to receive ten complaints a day alleging police brutality; after the Louima case, it began receiving twenty-five calls a day. The same phenomenon was experienced after the Rodney King beating in 1991. According to Joe Cook of the Dallas American Civil Liberties Union, the reason for the increase in calls is that, prior to the police abuse of King and Louima, people did not think anyone would take their stories of brutality seriously. "Now they hope someone will listen to them," Cook says.

Whether incidents such as the King and Louima beatings are isolated cases or part of a larger pattern of police misconduct is one of the issues considered in *Police Brutality: Current Controversies*. Also examined is the relationship between the police and the communities they serve—what causes the police to use excessive force on the very people they are supposed to be protecting, how the use of force affects community attitudes toward the police, and how police brutality can be prevented. Throughout this anthology, the authors debate the right of the individual to be free from harm versus society's interest in law and order.

Chapter 1

Is Police Brutality a Serious Problem?

Chapter Preface

Soon after Rudolph Giuliani became mayor of New York City in 1994, he began a crackdown on petty crime and criminals that reduced the rate of serious crime to levels the city had not experienced since the 1970s. While many of the city's residents were grateful for the increased police presence in their neighborhoods, others were less welcoming. Claims of police brutality increased 62 percent during the first two years of the crackdown. Other cities that instituted police crackdowns reported similar statistics—Cincinnati, Baltimore, Atlanta, Pittsburgh, and Washington, D.C., all recorded lower crime rates but a higher number of police brutality complaints. When newspapers reported in August 1997 that New York City police were alleged to have beaten and sodomized a Haitian immigrant named Abner Louima, critics of police seemed to be vindicated in their belief that police brutality was a common occurrence in police departments across the country.

Many civil rights groups—such as the American Civil Liberties Union and the National Association for the Advancement of Colored People—maintain that in their zeal to take back the streets from criminals, the police overstep the bounds of their authority by unnecessarily beating their suspects. Furthermore, these critics assert, this excessive use of force by some police officers is overlooked or condoned by their police departments. While these groups acknowledge that just a few officers are responsible for many of the brutality claims, they contend that the officers are rarely reprimanded or held accountable for their actions.

But others contend that the incidence of police brutality appears more widespread than it actually is due to national publicity over a few horrific cases. No national data on police brutality complaints are kept, so it is impossible to determine if allegations of brutality across the country are increasing, decreasing, or remaining the same. It is inevitable, police supporters argue, that there are more confrontations between civilians and police because there are more police on the street. Furthermore, in their rush to hire more police officers to fight crime, police departments inadequately screened or trained many of their officers. These poorly trained officers are more likely to be involved in disputes with civilians, supporters contend. But, they continue, once these new recruits gain a little experience in dealing with the public, the number of these conflicts should subside.

The extent of police brutality is not easily measured. Many factors must be considered when assessing the magnitude and seriousness of police use of force. In debating the seriousness of police brutality, the authors in the following chapter examine the role the media play in reporting police violence and the race and social status of the victims.

16

Police Brutality Is a Serious Problem

by Amnesty International

About the author: *Amnesty International is a worldwide voluntary movement that works to prevent governmental violations of people's fundamental human rights.*

Amnesty International (AI) has reviewed more than 90 individual cases of alleged ill-treatment and excessive force by New York City police officers, dating from the late 1980s to early 1996. The large majority of the cases involve officers from the New York Police Department (NYPD), although a few cases involve officers from the NYC Transit or Housing Authority Police Departments before their merger with the NYPD in 1995. In most cases civil lawsuits seeking damages for police misconduct were filed against the individual officers concerned, as well as against the Police Department and the City of New York as the authorities responsible for police practices and behaviour. These lawsuits include tort actions brought in the state courts, and cases brought under Title 42, Section 1983 of the United States Code (USC)—a federal civil rights statute which allows individuals to sue state officials directly in a state or federal court for violations of their civil or constitutional rights. In many of the cases examined substantial damages were awarded to the plaintiffs for alleged police misconduct. The police and other authorities have pointed out that civil lawsuits do not prove misconduct and that most cases are settled out-of-court by the city (i.e., without going to trial) without any admission of liability. However, Amnesty International was told that the city tends to settle cases where injuries or other evidence are consistent with the claims made. Many cases are settled on the basis of an independent evaluation of the facts by a judge, even if they do not go to trial. Amnesty International considers therefore that civil lawsuits provide an important source of information on the extent and nature of police misconduct. . . .

It is impossible to measure the full extent of police brutality from the data ex-

Excerpted from Amnesty International, *Police Brutality and Excessive Force in the New York City Police Department*, Section 2, "Summary of Amnesty International's Findings," subsections 2.1 and 2.9, June 1996, Index number AMR 51/36/96. Reprinted with permission.

amined. The sample of cases reviewed by AI represent only a small proportion of complaints filed against the police. They also represent a small proportion of encounters between the police and members of the public each year, most of which do not involve the use of force. However, the information collected suggests that police brutality and unnecessary force is nevertheless a widespread problem. The cases show a pattern of similar abuses occurring across the city, with minorities most at risk of being the victims of excessive force.

> *"An increase in complaints of unwarranted force [by police officers], leading to ill-treatment and deaths in custody, should be a matter of urgent concern."*

Furthermore, civil claims filed against New York City for police misconduct have been rising steadily for some years. A report prepared by the City Comptroller in February 1992 stated that the number of police misconduct claims filed with the Comptroller's Office had increased 53% over the five years from 1987 to 1991 (from just over 1,000 in 1987 to more than 1,500 in 1991). Claims have risen since then to around 2,000 annually. The number of actual lawsuits filed in any given year is somewhat lower but still substantial. More than 3,000 State and Federal civil lawsuits were brought against the City of New York alleging police misconduct for the years 1992 through 1995.

The number of cases actually disposed of in any given year is much lower, as civil lawsuits usually take years to reach a settlement. Statistics provided by the City Comptroller's Office show that damages have been awarded to victims of police misconduct in between 200 and 400 cases annually since 1988, as a result of out-of-court settlements or judgments in civil actions. The money paid out by the city in damages to alleged victims of police misconduct has risen from around $7 million in 1988 to more than $24 million in 1994.

Not an Accurate Measure

Some city counsel and police officials have suggested that the increase in civil actions is due to an increasingly litigious society and opportunistic lawyers prepared to file lawsuits in frivolous cases. However, it appears that civil lawsuits may in fact under-represent the true level of police misconduct. Attorneys and civil rights groups repeatedly told Amnesty International that many cases of ill-treatment did not result in lawsuits; these included cases where there were no independent witnesses; or the alleged victim was convicted of an offence arising out of the incident and had little chance of prevailing against the testimony of police officers; or the injuries were not severe enough to justify the costs involved in pursuing litigation. Although most such cases go unrecorded, this appeared to be borne out in some of the cases reviewed.

Complaints against the police lodged by members of the public with the Civilian Complaint Review Board (CCRB) have also risen sharply since 1993, despite reforms following the Mollen Commission of Inquiry. [The commission was established in 1992 by then-mayor David Dinkins to study police brutality in New York City.] The CCRB reported that it received 4,920 new complaints in 1994, an increase of 37.43% over the previous year. While the CCRB takes complaints covering a range of alleged abuses from deadly force to discourtesy, 1,670 complaints (the largest proportion) were for excessive force, and these had also risen proportionately from 1993. A further increase of 31.8% was noted for the first six months of 1995 (the last figures available) compared to the first six months of 1994.

Police Explanations

Police Commissioner William Bratton questioned the CCRB's statistics, stating that part of the increase was due to the merger of NYPD with the Transit and Housing police. However, these account for only a small proportion of the overall increase in complaints. Police officials have also suggested that the sharp increase in complaints was due to increased arrests and police activity during an intensive anti-crime drive in the city beginning in 1993 (known as the "quality of life initiative"), and that many complaints arose from more effective policing and an increase in arrests, rather than genuine abuses. The CCRB conceded in its reports that no firm conclusions could be drawn from the increases solely on the raw data on incoming complaints, and that part of the increase in complaints could be due to more civilian-police interactions during the anti-crime operations. However, they suggested that part of the increase could be due also to more awareness of the issue of police misconduct and publicity surrounding the creation of the new CCRB. They also noted that most of the complaints arose from encounters with patrol officers that did not involve arrests or persons receiving summonses and that "This would seem to discount the speculation that the increase is due to the increase in arrests resulting from the new quality-of-life initiatives". They noted also that most complainants had no prior complaint history, thus discounting suggestions that many of those lodging complaints were "chronic" complainers.

Deaths Caused by Police Increase

It is also noteworthy that the Police Department's own statistics for the same period show a rise in both the number of civilians who died from officers' firearms discharges and in the number of people who died while in police custody. These show a 34.8% increase in civilians shot dead in 1994 compared to 1993 (from 23 in 1993 to 31 in 1994) and a 53.3% increase in civilians who died in police custody (from 15 in 1993 to 23 in 1994). The figures also show an increase in the number of civilians injured from officers' firearms discharges during the same period (up from 54 to 60). Figures for 1995 were not available at the time of writing this report.

During their last visit to New York in November 1995, Amnesty International's delegates were told by several sources, including officials from the CCRB, that more aggressive policing in the past few years had led to an increase in complaints of ill-treatment. While effective measures to combat crime in New York City are obviously to be applauded, Amnesty International believes that an increase in complaints of unwarranted force, leading to ill-treatment and deaths in custody, should be a matter of urgent concern.

Brutality by Federal Law Enforcement Agents Is a Serious Problem

by Catherine M. Farmer

About the author: *Catherine M. Farmer is a freelance writer in Louisiana.*

"I love my country, but I'm afraid of my government." That's not just a slogan on the bumper stickers of a handful of radicals. It also reflects the sentiments of a growing number of thoughtful Americans.

A Renegade Government

In spite of bipartisan pledges of governmental accountability, many citizens are more concerned about assaults from federal agents than attacks from common criminals. Although lawful, for now the odds are not good when defending oneself from a renegade government. When Randy Weaver tried to protect his family in Ruby Ridge, Idaho, in 1992, from an unprovoked assault by some 400 federal agents, his wife Vickie, holding their baby in her arms, was shot through the head by a government sniper. Half her face was blown away. She died instantly. Their 14-year-old son Sammy was shot in the back and killed. The Branch Davidians' attempts at self-defense in Waco, Texas, in 1993, were also disastrous. Eighty-six women, children and men were killed. Some were shot to death; the rest were gassed and burned alive. In spite of the elaborate cover-up by the Clinton Administration, exhaustive documentation of FBI and Bureau of Alcohol, Tobacco and Firearms (ATF) treachery is becoming known. It's overwhelming.

As Paul Craig Roberts said in the *Washington Times*, "There is no longer any doubt that federal law enforcement agents committed illegal and unconstitutional acts in their bloody assaults on U.S. citizens at Waco, Texas, and Ruby Ridge, Idaho."

Although the Weaver and Branch Davidian atrocities were a turning point in

Reprinted from Catherine M. Farmer, "It's Time to Handcuff the Police," *Los Angeles Times*, April 26, 1995, by permission of the author.

the march toward government through terror, a pattern of unwarranted paramilitary assaults on Americans by various federal agencies is well-established. Testifying before a House Judiciary Committee, ATF Director Stephen Higgins noted that hundreds of "activations" similar to the Waco attack were routinely employed by his agency. Moreover, 10 public policy organizations, including the National Association of Defense Lawyers and the American Civil Liberties Union (ACLU), have documented "widespread abuses of civil liberties and human rights" committed by federal agencies. In a paper presented at the annual conference of the American Society of Criminology in November, 1994, David Kopel and Paul H. Blackman point out that while "it might be hoped that the Randy Weaver and Waco disasters would prompt a cutback in federal military-style strike forces intended for use against Americans, just the opposite has happened."

Federal Police and the Constitution

There are only two references to a specific need for federal police action in our Constitution: "To provide for the punishment of counterfeiting the securities and current coin of the United States" and "to define and punish piracies and felonies committed on the high seas and offenses against the law of nations." Nevertheless, extraordinary federal police powers of questionable constitutionality have evolved from the "necessary and proper clause," the interstate commerce power and the taxing power. We are reaping the whirlwind. If we are to survive as a free people, we must curtail the size and power of federal law enforcement.

> *"A pattern of unwarranted paramilitary assaults on Americans by various federal agencies is well-established."*

Roughly 79,000 law enforcement officers work for the federal government—almost 10% of the country's law enforcement personnel. Fifty-three separate agencies are authorized to carry firearms and make arrests. Since the Weaver and Branch Davidian debacles, the U.S. Marshal Service has added a new 100-person "Special Operations Group" and the FBI Hostage Rescue Team (of Waco fame) has expanded to 150. And thanks to exemptions in the Posse Comitatus Act, by alleging drug violations, federal agencies can access the equipment and manpower of the United States military.

Law Enforcement Is Increasingly Militarized

"Spurred by the 'drug war,'" warn Kopel and Blackman, "law enforcement in the United States, particularly federal law enforcement, has become increasingly militarized. No-knock raids with battering rams, agents dressed like ninjas and spray-firing machine guns, the fabrication of information in warrant application, forfeiture and confiscation of property without a trial and a steadily blurring distinction between the standards appropriate for law enforcement in a free society and the practices typical of military occupation of a conquered nation have been the most important law enforcement trend of the last decade." Undoubtedly, the reprehensible 1995 Oklahoma City bombing will exacerbate this trend.

The brutality and lawlessness of federal law enforcement agencies are real. They do not, however, justify brutality and lawlessness from our citizenry. It's not too late to avoid totalitarianism or anarchy. Our Constitution and the rule of law can quash them both.

Police Brutality Against Minorities Is a Serious Problem

by Bernice Powell Jackson

About the author: *Bernice Powell Jackson is the executive director of the United Church of Christ Commission for Racial Justice and a columnist for the on-line publication* Black World Today.

In New York City two Hispanic men are killed when they are shot from behind 28 times and another Hispanic man is choked to death after his football hits a police car. In Pittsburgh, an African American businessman is choked to death after being stopped for a traffic violation. A St. Petersburg, Florida, African American motorist is shot to death also after a traffic stop. A New Haven, Connecticut, African American man suffers the same fate. In each case the killing occurred while the men were in police custody or in the course of a police action.

These are just a few of the stories which were heard at the National Emergency Conference on Police Brutality held in New York City in 1997. Sponsored by the Center for Constitutional Rights, this conference brought together people who had experienced police brutality from across the nation, including Kentucky, Georgia, Ohio, Florida, New York, and New Jersey.

The Criminal Injustice System

Indeed, criminal justice is the issue which seems to show the greatest racial divide in this nation. Most people of color would characterize the system as the criminal injustice system and most European Americans would not. A *New York Times* columnist wrote how, in the course of writing a book, he has asked African American men across the nation whether they have ever been hassled by police. Most of them can tell a story of being stopped in a store or in their car while driving in a white neighborhood. Some may have been questioned

Reprinted from Bernice Powell Jackson, "Civil Rights Journal: Justice Denied; Police Brutality and Us," *Oakland Post*, May 14, 1997, by permission of the author.

simply because they were at a phone booth or in a mall. It doesn't matter whether they are well-dressed or what their occupation. Even off-duty or plain-clothes police officers have been stopped, or occasionally even shot while on duty. Few European American men have had this experience.

Not only are hundreds, perhaps thousands of people of color victims of police brutality every year, but they seldom find justice in the courts. Take the case of Jonny Gammage, an African American businessman and the cousin of Pittsburgh Steelers player Ray Seals. Mr. Gammage was choked to death after a routine traffic stop outside Pittsburgh in 1995. In April 1997, the judge in the case dismissed charges against the police officers accused in his killing, saying that prosecutors unfairly singled them out.

> *"Not only are hundreds, perhaps thousands of people of color victims of police brutality every year, but they seldom find justice in the courts."*

Or take the case of Anthony Baez, the young New Yorker who was choked by police after his football hit a patrol car. The officer accused in his murder was acquitted of all charges in a non-jury trial.

Others Are Victims, Too

It is important to note that while police brutality disproportionately impacts communities of color that the number of European American victims is growing. A *Montel Williams* show focused on white victims, for instance. And it is also important to note that while most of the police officers are European American, there are officers of color who occasionally have been found to be violent.

Finally it should be noted that brutality is not just found in police officers. It is also present in corrections officers, immigration officers and others in the criminal justice system. And its victims are also women, often those who are incarcerated.

Police Brutality Against Hispanics Is a Serious Problem

by Michael Huspek

About the author: *Michael Huspek is an associate professor of communications at California State University in San Marcos.*

A report by the San Diego office of the American Friends Service Committee (AFSC) reveals 267 complaints of human and civil rights violations suffered by persons at the hands of law enforcement officials in and around San Diego, California. While the complaints involve the Sheriff's Department in Vista, San Marcos and Fallbrook, the San Diego Police Department and the California Highway Patrol, those agencies most frequently singled out are U.S. Customs and the Immigration and Naturalization Service (INS), including the Border Patrol.

Among the complaints are 63 narratives, recorded over a three-year period, that provide a uniquely human look at how law enforcement agencies may be operating on the edge of lawlessness. Among the complaints are: illegal stops and searches of persons and their private property; verbal, psychological and physical abuse; deprivation of food, water and medical attention; and use of excessive force.

Illegal Immigrants

The narratives represent a highly diverse population. This includes undocumented immigrants such as Jorge Soriano Bautista who, detected entering the United States without legal documentation, ran from the Border Patrol until he was hit hard in the back by an agent's Ford Bronco, knocking him to the ground and causing him to black out.

Upon regaining consciousness, Bautista heard his arm snap while being handcuffed, and he again blacked out. Bautista was given no medical attention for either his broken arm or the blow to his body caused by the Bronco. Instead, he

Reprinted from Michael Huspek, "Law and Lawlessness in San Diego," *San Diego Union-Tribune*, February 26, 1998, by permission of the author.

was hauled to the border and stuffed by agents back under the fence onto the Mexican side.

Legal Residents Are Also Under Attack

Many of the narratives are also voiced by legal residents and citizens of the United States. Consider Abel Arroyo, a 19-year-old U.S. citizen who attended the San Diego Regional Center for the Developmentally Disabled. Attempting to pass through the San Ysidro Port of Entry after a brief shopping trip to Tijuana, Arroyo declared his U.S. citizenship and showed his birth certificate, state ID and social security card.

INS agents refused to believe him, however. In fact, one of the agents taunted Arroyo, hurled racial insults at him and then punched him in the stomach. For seven hours he pleaded with officers to be allowed entry, but to no avail. Without identity documents, he then wandered the streets of Tijuana for days until he met a man who agreed to smuggle him across the border for a fee. Eleven days after being denied entry into his own country, Arroyo was smuggled across the border and reunited with his family.

Complaints Have Increased

The INS has not been altogether oblivious to complaints such as these. In January 1998, John Chase, head of the INS Office of Internal Audit (OIA), announced that public complaints to the INS had risen 29 percent from 1996, with the "vast majority" emanating from the southwest border region.

More than 2,300 complaints were filed in 1997 as opposed to the 1,813 complaints filed in 1996. An additional 400 reports of "minor misconduct" were placed in a new category that previously had not been used. Chase emphasized, however, that the 243 "serious" allegations of abuse and use of excessive force that could warrant criminal prosecution were down in 1997 as compared to the 328 in 1996. These "serious" cases are considered distinct from "less serious" complaints such as "verbal abuse, discrimination, extended detention without cause."

"Given that . . . the complaints in the . . . study are voiced by persons of Hispanic descent, a most obvious inference is that law enforcement . . . is being applied discriminatorily."

On the same day that Chase spoke to the public, the INS issued a spate of press releases detailing an action plan that is meant to increase the information being made available to the public, expand dialogue between INS and community groups, enhance dissemination of INS information, increase public knowledge about complaint procedures, improve complaint process case management and incorporate local community-based training of INS staff.

Such changes are to be commended. Better training and monitoring of agents is sorely needed as they are being deployed in the field at an unprecedented rate. And with a steady rise in state funding, coupled with increasing points of contact between agents and the public, it is essential that the community have a better understanding of the application, logic and effects of law enforcement practices. Such measures, moreover, need to be implemented by U.S. Customs and all other law enforcement agencies, as well as the INS.

An External Review Board Is Needed

Nevertheless, such proposed changes do not go far enough in the right direction. Most vitally needed is an external review board—with genuine citizen participatory input—that can objectively determine the validity of complaints. This need is patent in light of the track records of the two offices most responsible for dealing with public complaints: the INS' OIA and the Office of the U.S. Attorney of the Southern District.

> *"The number and frequency of complaints are enough to suggest that law enforcement practices are being applied discriminatorily."*

Complaints appear to be routinely swept under the carpet within the OIA. And the U.S. Attorney's Office does no better. Of the 63 AFSC-assisted complaints filed at different times over the 1995–1997 period, all received back an identical form letter stating: "After careful review . . . we have concluded that there is insufficient evidence to establish a prosecutable violation of the federal criminal civil rights statutes."

Discriminatory Practices

Beyond institution of an external review board, further discussion needs to be devoted to the frequency and nature of abuses being committed by law enforcement personnel. Given that virtually all of the complaints in the AFSC study are voiced by persons of Hispanic descent, a most obvious inference is that law enforcement in the southwest region is being applied discriminatorily.

This is not to state that all law enforcement practices are racially motivated; nor is it to claim that all agents who engage in such practices are driven by racist sentiments. Yet the number and frequency of complaints are enough to suggest that law enforcement practices are being applied discriminatorily.

The current process of distinguishing "serious" abuses such as rapes or shootings from "less serious" abuses is inadequate. Verbal abuse, discrimination and extended detention without cause must be treated as the crimes that they are. What distinguishes the verbal abuse that frequently accompanies excessive use of force by law enforcement officials from hate crimes?

In an atmosphere where immigrant strawberry pickers have been sighted between the cross-hairs of an intensified criminalization strategy, it seems fitting that law enforcement officials' violations of the law also be treated as crimes and not merely as forms of institutional misconduct.

Chapter 1

We grant to our law enforcement agencies an enormous responsibility, including the right to authoritatively intervene into our lives. There are boundaries that cannot be transgressed, however. The law is not to be enforced arbitrarily; nor is it to be enforced selectively against some but not others. Above all, law enforcement officials cannot abrogate subjects' human and civil rights. To do so constitutes a breaking of the law that instills terror in us all.

Brutality Against Prisoners Is a Serious Problem

by Ben Chaney and Karen Carrillo

About the authors: *Ben Chaney is the director of the James Earl Chaney Foundation, a civil rights organization named for Ben Chaney's brother, a civil rights activist who was killed in 1964 in Mississippi. Karen Carrillo is a regional editor of* Third Force *magazine and the deputy editor of* City Sun *in Brooklyn, New York.*

Andre Lamond Jones was an 18-year-old African American teenager scheduled to go to college in the fall of 1992. In August 1992, Andre—the son of Esther Jones-Quinn, president of the Jackson, Mississippi, chapter of the National Association for the Advancement of Colored People (NAACP), and the stepson of Minister Charles X Quinn, the local Jackson leader of the Nation of Islam—was driving his girlfriend home from a date when he was stopped by an officer from the Brandon County Sheriff's Department. Jones was arrested for having an open beer can in the front seat, carrying a concealed weapon and allegedly altering the vehicle identification number of the truck he was driving.

Hanged with a Shoestring

He was first taken to the Brandon County Jail and later transferred to nearby Simpson County Jail. But within hours of being moved, 18-year-old, five-foot-nine-inch Andre Lamond Jones was found hanging from a nine-foot shower stall with his Nike shoelaces wrapped around his neck.

The Mississippi state medical examiner ruled Jones' death a suicide. But Chicago pathologist Dr. James Bryant, who later conducted an autopsy on Jones, concluded that it was physically impossible for a person to pick himself up by a shoestring and hang himself from the rafters of a shower stall without the aid of a chair or stool—neither of which were in the young man's cell. "Someone in the jail killed him," Bryant told a reporter. "And whoever killed him took the body and hung it to make it look like a suicide."

Jones' case is hardly unique. Cedric Walker, a Black, 23-year-old asthmatic,

Reprinted from Ben Chaney and Karen Carrillo, "Under Color of Law: Mississippi Jailhouse Deaths and the Struggle for Human Rights," *Third Force*, September/October 1995, by permission of *Third Force*.

was incarcerated at Mississippi's Parchman Correctional Facility, a penitentiary reserved for the state's most hardened criminals. Even though doctors at another prison had previously diagnosed Walker as a severe asthmatic, when he was transferred to the tougher Parchman facility, he was reportedly beaten on several occasions by guards who became annoyed with his requests for medication.

> *"There are too many people dying while incarcerated in Mississippi."*

Walker wrote letters home complaining about how he was being treated at Parchman: "I'm sick right now and I'm getting tired of this shit," he wrote to his fiancée, Juanita Lee, on August 11, 1992. "I keep getting sick and these people don't care whether you get sick or not."

On the night of his death, witnesses say they saw Walker in the prison infirmary with three guards. Prison reports also show that Walker had been taken to the clinic for emergency asthma treatment, but that instead of receiving medical care the official prison incident report and some of Walker's fellow prisoners say he was carried back to his cell and "beaten down."

The next morning, Cedric Walker was found in his Parchman cell with one end of a rope wrapped around his neck and the other end tied to a window knob. Prison officials concluded that Walker had somehow managed to hang himself by tying the rope around his neck and leaning forward while sitting upright in his bed.

A number of witnesses, however, quickly came forward to tell another story. According to accounts from other prisoners, detailed in letters sent to Walker's family, Walker was seriously mistreated at the prison clinic. A number of prisoners also say that they heard a scuffle break out between Walker and the guards who returned him to his cell the night he died. . . .

Statements from the medical examiner eventually confirmed the report submitted by the Mississippi Highway Patrol (MHP) officer stationed at Parchman, who claimed to have interviewed prisoners who had information about Cedric's death, but still ruled the death a suicide. The MHP report was forwarded to the Mississippi office of the FBI and then to the Justice Department in Washington, D.C., where the Cedric Walker case was officially closed.

Yet all the witnesses who wrote Cedric Walker's family say that no one from the FBI or MHP ever interviewed them.

Old Times Are Not Forgotten

Mississippi, the state with this country's most vicious history of racial violence and oppression, is once again the focus of activists who want the federal government to step in and take over a criminal justice system that seems out of control. Since 1987 the New York–based Chaney Foundation has documented more than 57 mysterious deaths in Mississippi's jails and prisons, 48 of which

31

involved hangings. Of those hanging deaths, 25 were Black men.

While many of the deaths have been officially labeled suicides or escape attempts, the explanations for the missing and dead victims just don't add up: There are too many people dying while incarcerated in Mississippi. Activists believe that the deaths are murders, committed by—or at the very least sanctioned by—law enforcement officers with the purpose of enforcing the state's historically repressive white supremacist social order.

Blatant Racism

If there is a state that has symbolized American racism at its most blatant, it is Mississippi. The 1964 Mississippi Freedom Summer deaths of civil rights activists James Earl Chaney, Andrew Goodman and Michael Schwerner weren't even the first of Mississippi's atrocities to receive national attention. But because they featured the first deaths of Northern white civil rights workers, they garnered the attention and resources of the national media and federal authorities in a way no Black deaths ever had.

The Freedom Summer murders gave such a bad name to Mississippi in the '60s that the state's public relations machinery has been working overtime to promote a more moderate image of its state authorities ever since. Unfortunately, many local activists report the new image is not to be believed.

"After World War II, in the long dark night of Mississippi's massive resistance to the Second Reconstruction, a resurgent tradition of unpunished white vigilantism brought new infamy to the state, reaffirming its reputation as 'the land of the tree and the home of the grave,'" wrote Neil R. McMillen in his book *Dark Journey: Black Mississippians in the Age of Jim Crow.*

The white vigilantism that made Mississippi notorious during the civil rights era was essentially a commingling of local police forces with members of the Ku Klux Klan and other white supremacy adherents. As many civil rights historians have documented, law enforcement authorities in small towns and cities across the state knew of and often held membership in local white hate groups. In the early part of this century, lynchings and white-sheet terrorism were given such free reign in Mississippi that in the heyday of the NAACP's activism and organizing years—when the group initiated federal lawsuits against segregation and opened chapters across the South full of members ready to walk picket lines and suffer the potentially violent dangers of sit-ins—the most powerful civil rights organization in the country was itself only able to operate skeletal chapters in what they termed "the Savage State."

Uninterested Media

"Mississippi has for the past two generations, since the death of Emmett Till, escaped the censure of the rest of the country because of its ability to manipulate the press," says Charles Tisdale, publisher of the *Jackson Advocate.*

The *Jackson Advocate,* Mississippi's largest Black newspaper, was the first paper to report on the jail hangings. Tisdale wrote a number of Op-Ed columns that identified these deaths as part of a pattern of official misconduct. "I have long been concerned about human rights abuses in Mississippi," Tisdale said in 1993. "[And] the complicity of public officials, especially district attorneys and the press, to suppress news about African Americans that's not easy to take, [like] the lynchings such as the ones that have occurred currently and other human rights abuses."

But while Tisdale's articles pointed out what many Mississippians may have already suspected, most of the local and national media seemed uninterested in stories about suspicious deaths of prisoners. Some members of the African American community began to try to raise public awareness around the issue during the early 1990s. Individually, the families of those prisoners who had mysteriously died petitioned lawyers, state authorities and even the federal government to investigate, but they had few resources and virtually no hard information to go on—only personal convictions.

"I know he was murdered," says Esther Quinn about her son Andre Jones.

"Hearings established a pattern for Mississippi's 'jailhouse suicides': a suspect is arrested on minor charges . . . but becomes so despondent that he . . . commits suicide."

"He was a stable, self-confident person with very high self-esteem, in good spirits. He was going to enroll in college (at Alcorn State) the next day." Dissatisfied with the official explanations for Jones' death, a local clergy group began to speak out and suggested that one factor that may have led to Jones' death was the absence of Black deputies in Simpson County.

The Jones case eventually began to receive some national attention—no doubt, partly because of the political credentials of his parents—after being featured in *Jet* magazine and in the Nation of Islam's *Final Call.* As the story of Andre Jones' death was covered in the *Final Call,* many Nation of Islam members voiced concern about the plight of African Americans in Mississippi and Minister Louis Farrakhan paid a visit to the state, threatening that if the truth was not uncovered in this case, the Nation would have to do its own investigation. . . .

The Hearings

In April 1992 prominent members of Mississippi's African American community called on Ben Chaney to support them in trying to investigate what was being called the "jailhouse suicides." Chaney, who was living in New York and had established the James Earl Chaney Foundation in memory of his late brother, was initially reluctant. He suggested that it would be more advantageous for the community to contact more noted prisoners' and civil rights organizations, because they would have more resources to investigate the deaths. Finally, a call from Charles Tisdale brought Ben Chaney back to Mississippi, a state he and his family left in fear soon after the death of his brother.

After a preliminary investigation, the James Earl Chaney Foundation quickly sponsored the Commission of Human Rights Abuse in Mississippi hearings. . . .

The purpose of the March 1993 hearings was to examine jailhouse and other mysterious deaths in the state.

The hearings established a pattern for Mississippi's "jailhouse suicides": a suspect is arrested on minor charges—usually a traffic violation—but becomes so despondent that he contemplates and then commits suicide. No one hears or sees anything during the time the suicide occurs, but later, unexplained injuries are discovered on the victim's body. Police reports about how the victims killed themselves tend to involve them having the ability to perform amazing acrobatics and contortionist moves that the victims' families were unaware of.

Guilty of the Cardinal Sin

In the case of many Black victims, allegations would surface soon after their deaths that the "suicide" victim had been dating a white woman. While Mississippi has resolved many of its more overt racial problems, there are still sections and whole counties in the state where Jim Crow is quietly still the norm and any ideas about interracial dating are out of the question.

"I talked to Scott," says David Scott Campbell's father, M.C., about his concern that his African American son was dating a white woman. "I told him, 'Scott, you got to stop [dating white women]. If you don't, it's going to get you in trouble. . . . They'll mess you up real bad.'" Scott Campbell was found hanging in his cell, strung up by the leg of his pants, after being arrested on his 21st birthday. "I'll go to my grave saying he didn't commit suicide," Campbell's father says.

Scott Campbell's body was discovered by officer Dicky Sistrunk, one of the officers who first arrested Campbell. According to Sistrunk, times have changed in Mississippi, even though he acknowledges that interracial sex is still viewed as a "cardinal sin." Dating a Black guy might earn a white girl a beating from her father, says Sistrunk, but he also asserts that in the new Mississippi, it's not something anyone would get killed over. "My personal belief is if they want to mix up . . . that's their business. It doesn't mean I have to jump right in and do the same," he says. Ironically, Sistrunk, in stereotypical Southern lawman fashion, repeatedly refers to Campbell—just three years his junior at the time of his death—as "that boy."

> *"Race was clearly not the only issue in which law enforcement abuses were concerned."*

As might be expected, the hearings were roundly criticized by Mississippi state and local law enforcement officers. "Anything happens here, and it's always made out to be the worst that it could possibly be," said Glenn Waddell, the sheriff in Neshoba County, where David Scott Campbell was found dead. Jim Ingram, Mississippi public safety commissioner and an FBI agent during the civil rights era, has complete faith in the final determination presented by his former employer. "The deaths brought up by the commission all were investigated by the FBI, which found that they were suicides and that there was no basis for any suspicion of murder," he says. Of course, activists already concerned about the possibility of law enforcement involvement in the deaths are not so easily convinced.

> *"Constant exposure and ongoing documentation of law enforcement abuses might someday help to end questionable prisoner deaths in Mississippi."*

The hearings, while primarily focused on jail hangings of Black inmates, also revealed that race was clearly not the only issue in which law enforcement abuses were concerned. Several relatives of white hanging victims also insist that their family members were murdered. "The issue of abuse and jail hangings are not a racial issue," says Andrea Gibbs, a former deputy sheriff in Harrison County, Mississippi. Gibbs blew the whistle on the abuse of juvenile prisoners in the state—and lost her job for her efforts. "There are just as many white people who've been beaten [and killed]." Gibbs worked for one year at the Harrison County Youth Detention Center, where she claims to have personally witnessed the beatings of 12 youth inmates.

"People think the Civil Rights Movement just ended, and that's it," Gibbs says. But the Council of Federated Organization's (COFO) Mississippi Freedom Summer Project was meant to have long-term goals, she asserts. "All I wanted was to just stop the beatings at juvenile detention centers. I was naive enough to think that exposing this would begin to right all the wrongs.". . .

The Deaths Continue

With little national attention paid to these deaths, Mississippi activists are pushing ahead, trying to keep information about jailhouse and prison deaths constantly in the news. . . .

Since 1991 more than 40 people have been beaten while in the custody of the Hattiesburg police. More than half of those beaten have suffered severe trauma as a result of the abuse. Most of the victims were stopped for minor traffic violations, disorderly conduct or some other minor infraction, but then abused and later released. In many instances the initial charges were later dropped. Some of the victims were elderly, many were Black, most were poor and/or unemployed. . . .

Constant exposure and ongoing documentation of law enforcement abuses might someday help to end questionable prisoner deaths in Mississippi.

Meanwhile, for many residents of Mississippi, especially the families of prisoners whose jail deaths are listed as suicides, there will continue to be many unanswered questions and frustrations about the treatment of prisoners. They fear that the "new Mississippi" is just a slicker and more sophisticated version of the Mississippi of the 1950s.

The Media Downplay Police Brutality

by *Revolutionary Worker*

About the author: Revolutionary Worker *is a newspaper published by the Revolutionary Communist Party.*

On the morning of August 9, 1997, Abner Louima was beaten and raped with the handle of a toilet plunger in a New York police station. At least four cops beat him. The main cop who raped Abner Louima paraded around the stationhouse like a maniac, waving the plunger he was going to use. He shouted, "This is Giuliani time," as he carried out his sick and brutal deeds. [Rudolph Giuliani is the mayor of New York City.]

Looking the Other Way

Not a single cop in the stationhouse responded to Abner Louima's screams. Not a single cop lifted a finger to accompany Abner Louima to the emergency room, even though they knew that he was suffering severely and in possible danger of death. A nurse at the hospital where the cops took Louima was overheard to say that *this time* she couldn't go along with it and lie for them. Later the police commissioner said that he was shocked because "this wasn't brutality, this was criminal"—as if brutality is not a crime. And of the nearly 100 cops at the precinct who have been interviewed on this, *only two* have come forward to say a single word.

The Lessons Are Clear

The lessons of this should seem clear to anyone:

• *At a minimum,* that there are extremely sick and brutal cops on the New York police force who run rampant.

• At a minimum, that the leadership of the department does not consider police brutality to be a crime, and almost all the officers will go to great lengths, including perjury, to cover up even the worst, most murderous instance of it.

• That there is very likely an ongoing, business-as-usual conspiracy between

Reprinted from the September 21, 1997, *Revolutionary Worker* editorial, "Police Torture of Abner Louima: Lies, Damn Lies, . . . and the System's Damage Control," by permission of the *Revolutionary Worker*. Subheadings, a new title, and the inserted quotation have been added to the original text by Greenhaven editors.

police and the city hospital system to cover up severe cases of it.

• To top it off, that the police understand their most brutal and sadistic actions to be part of Mayor Giuliani's program.

Any ordinary person, no matter how cut off from reality, must now consider the evidence that there is in fact an epidemic of police brutality, and must at least wonder whether police brutality and murder are just "business as usual" these days.

But the major media are promoting a different set of lessons.

On August 29, 1997, ABC *World News Tonight* covered the demonstra-

> *"[The media] are drumming into people that what happened . . . is an 'isolated incident' and that the police themselves are already taking care of the problem."*

tion of over 5,000 people in New York against police brutality. They gave the demonstration literally a few seconds, before getting to the "meat" of their story—that in other cities, the people who are putting a stop to police brutality are . . . the police! Yes, ABC decided that the main thing people needed to know about were the supposed efforts of the Los Angeles or New Orleans police departments to root out brutality and corruption. (Somehow Mayor Giuliani's similar program, called CPR—Courtesy, Professionalism and Respect—was not covered.)

The September 1, 1997, *Time* magazine played another chorus of the exact same song. To quote *Time:* "Headlines about brutality have overshadowed the real news: more cities are reining in police misbehavior." And they, too, went on to focus on the wonders of the born-again LAPD.

Media Whitewash

Too bad they didn't get around to interviewing the Gutierrez family. They could have told *Time* about how their 14-year-old son Jose Antonio was shot in the back and killed in cold blood in 1995 by the LAPD. They could have told *Time* how just this past July [1997] Antonio's mother, Ana Maria Gutierrez, was arrested and brutalized by the LAPD over a bogus traffic violation.

On one level, this media whitewash calls to mind the old Richard Pryor line—"who you gonna believe, me or your lying eyes?" It is ridiculous and pitiful double-talk of someone caught in the act.

On another level, we must take this very seriously. They are drumming into people that what happened to Abner Louima is an "isolated incident" and that the police themselves are already taking care of the problem. They are telling middle-class people in particular to forget about the whole nightmare and go back to sleep, to let *them* "handle the situation." And they are letting us know that they intend to whitewash this, and that they may very well decide to even set Abner Louima's attackers free. After all, they have a whole program at stake here—a whole way they intend to control social upheaval and deepening divisions in society—and they are going to use everything at their command to keep it together.

Fight for Justice

We cannot allow this. We have to get the real story out, relying on ourselves and our actions. We will have to fight tooth and nail for justice for Abner Louima, *and* we will have to unite everyone we can to get the real meaning of this case out there: that police brutality and repression is an epidemic and that it will take the massive resistance of the people to stop it.

The Extent of Police Brutality Is Exaggerated

by William J. Bratton

About the author: *William J. Bratton, the New York City police commissioner from 1994 to 1996, is the president of First Security Consulting.*

The arrest of four New York City police officers in the alleged August 1997 torture of Abner Louima, a Haitian immigrant, reopens an old debate. Has the Police Department's sharper focus on community policing and quality-of-life crimes led officers to abuse their authority and use excessive force? Have we paid too high a price for the remarkable decline in crime that has occurred since 1993?

Not a Large Problem

The answer is no. This incident does not reflect a larger problem with the police force. In fact, such horror stories rarely occur. A 1994 study by the New York City Police Department found that although officers made nearly 275,000 arrests in 1993, fewer than 100 people were hospitalized as a result of these encounters. This number includes people who violently resisted arrest—including those who shot at officers.

Civilian complaints are also often misrepresented. The peak year for civilian complaints against the Police Department was 1985; there were 7,073 complaints, 26 percent more than in 1996.

This peak followed a period of heavy hiring in the early 1980's, as the department began to make up for the layoffs caused by the 1975 fiscal crisis.

Indeed, complaints always rise after there is a large influx of new police officers. In 1992, when Mayor David Dinkins hired thousands of officers under his Safe Streets, Safe City program, complaints rose. And complaints continued to rise during Mayor Rudolph Giuliani's term. Once again, the Police Department was absorbing new officers: the Safe Streets program hired 4,000 more officers, and about 6,000 Transit and Housing Authority officers joined the rolls, as the three police agencies were combined into one.

Why do complaints rise when large numbers of officers are hired? Experience in city after city confirms that rookie officers need seasoning to learn how to exert authority without offending or fighting with people.

The Police Department in Birmingham, Ala., for example, hired its largest rookie class ever in 1994. A year later, there was a 70 percent increase in civilian complaints, even though 60 percent of the officers were black. In 1996, as the officers grew more experienced, the number of complaints declined by almost 70 percent.

> *"[One] incident does not reflect a larger problem with the police force."*

In New York City, the number of complaints to the Civilian Complaint Review Board declined by 20 percent in the first six months of 1997 when compared with the same period in 1996. But this decline still doesn't placate the department's critics. When complaints were rising, they blamed police brutality. When complaints declined, they argued that the public had no faith in the independent board, and therefore did not bother filing complaints. Sorry, the critics can't have it both ways.

Of course, the department should not retreat from its efforts to reduce police brutality. It must continue to improve and expand its screening of recruits, as well as its training and supervision of officers.

Community Policing Reduces Crime

But the case of Abner Louima should not undermine the reputation or change the assertive tactics of the New York City Police Department. Consider the turnaround that has been accomplished in New York City. Crime is down by more than 50 percent from 1990. Murders are down by 63 percent. There will be 200,000 fewer victims of major crimes in 1997 than there were in 1990.

These successes didn't just happen. They were achieved by embracing the concept of community policing, including the emphasis on partnership, problem solving, prevention and developing a consensus in neighborhoods about what constitutes appropriate behavior.

Fear, disorderly conduct and crime divide communities and threaten urban life. Restoring order and reducing crime are basic to a civil, democratic society.

The Use of Extreme Force Is Sometimes Justified

by Sarah J. McCarthy

About the author: *Sarah J. McCarthy is a freelance writer.*

Jonny Gammage died on the night of October 12, 1995, in front of Frank and Shirley's pancake parlor, just three miles from my home. Jonny was a black man, a cousin and business partner of Pittsburgh Steeler Ray Seals, and he died in the custody of five white suburban policemen who had pulled him over for a minor traffic violation. Gammage's last words, according to Whitehall police Sgt. Keith Henderson, were the unforgettable words of a man who feared for his life. "Keith, Keith, I'm only 31," he begged as he lay prone on the ground, the officers holding him down. A few minutes later he was dead of suffocation from the pressure applied to his neck and chest.

Creating an Explosive Situation

Sgt. Henderson testified that Gammage came out of the car swinging, and that had he been the arresting officer he would have shot Gammage. An eyewitness tow truck driver, sitting in Frank and Shirley's parking lot, refuted the officer's testimony, saying that a Brentwood policeman initiated the altercation, attacking Gammage from behind. One of the cops had a suspicious violent act in his past, and Jonny Gammage had a couple alleged incidents, inadmissible in court, where he had been belligerent to police officers in Syracuse.

Though there is no agreement on what really happened that night, two things are certain. Gammage shouldn't have died during a routine traffic stop, and the mutual demonization process that smolders between blacks and whites—especially between black men and white cops—created an explosive situation.

Fortunately, as we go to press, violence has not followed the acquittal in November 1996 of one of the white police officers charged with wrongdoing in Gammage's death. The Reverend Jesse Jackson did call Gammage's death a "lynching," and demonstrators outside the county courthouse did protest the all-white jury that acquitted the officer, but so far the city has escaped the kind of

Reprinted from Sarah J. McCarthy, "Letter from Pittsburgh," *Chronicles*, January 1997, by permission of *Chronicles*.

rioting seen recently in St. Petersburg, Florida.

The "officer dragged case," as it's known in Pittsburgh, is equally explosive. It involves John Wilbur, a police officer who in 1996 was dragged through the city streets by his hand by a car full of black juveniles careening at speeds of up to 71 m.p.h.

Officer Wilbur had first approached the stolen car because three black teenagers were stopped in the middle of the street, sleeping at 1:30 A.M. at a green light. Wilbur opened the rear door of the champagne-colored Honda Accord after he saw one of the boys pop something into his mouth, which Wilbur correctly thought was drugs. The teenager slammed the door on Wilbur's hand. "I knew my hand was stuck in the door and I was going with this car whether I wanted to or not," Wilbur testified later from his wheelchair.

Dragged bouncing through the streets, Wilbur described the terror of traffic whizzing by in the opposite direction and the red flashes of police cars chasing behind him. The pain in his hand, his feet and his leg—which was scraped to the bone—was horrendous, but with three giant steps Wilbur vaulted himself atop the trunk of the car, reached for his gun with his free right hand and blindly fired at the occupants, killing two of them. The third, the driver, stopped the car and fled into the night.

> *"Anybody being dragged at 71 m.p.h. down the street for almost a mile has and should have the right to protect himself against those people."*

Luckily for Wilbur, there were several witnesses to the incident who contradicted the accusations that spewed from the black community. Of the many verbal assaults on Wilbur, perhaps the worst was from Homewood resident Adama Taylor. "Wilbur deserved to get dragged up the street," she yelled at a police civilian review board meeting, "and I wish like hell his legs were broke the hell off. For real!"

Incredibly, despite the testimony of eyewitnesses backing Wilbur's account of the incident, four out of six of the jurors at the coroner's inquest said Wilbur should be arrested. The three black jurors said Wilbur should be charged with manslaughter for the deaths of the two youths, and one white juror wanted Wilbur held for homicide. The remaining two white female jurors thought Wilbur's actions were justified.

Allegheny County District Attorney Robert Colville refused to charge Wilbur, despite the findings of the coroner's jury, saying: "The law is clear. Anybody being dragged at 71 m.p.h. down the street for almost a mile has and should have the right to protect himself against those people."

Racial Demonization

The Gammage and Wilbur cases illustrate the atmosphere of racial demonization that permeates American culture. Although blacks have been the historical victims of racial demonization, today the demonization of whites in America

42

has evolved to the point that black juries are increasingly finding black skin an entitlement to victim status, whether one has dragged a cop through the streets or cut off a woman's head.

Valerie McDonald, an African-American on Pittsburgh's City Council, responding to black reactions to the "officer dragged case," said she was glad Pittsburgh got to "hear the outrage" from the black community. "I'm happy that you felt discomfort, very edgy on your seat," she stated, her voice rising. "You needed to hear the anger that's going on in the community. Not everybody in Pittsburgh is happy."

Ms. McDonald also recently defended Pittsburgh's drug dealers, claiming that these boys are just selling drugs to put "meat and potatoes" on the family table. Just in case young black males need any additional encouragement to deal drugs, carjack, or drag policemen through the streets by their hands, there's always a hallelujah chorus who will provide the excuses and lead the cheers.

It is understandable that McDonald and others who care about young black males would want to blame someone outside the community for the destruction and chaos in their lives. It is understandable, but definitely not helpful to these boys who are in ever-increasing numbers ending up murdered, addicted, or in jail—not because of racist cops, but because of the crime spree in which they are so heavily involved.

"One black male graduates from college for every 100 who go to jail," stated General Colin Powell at a recent graduation speech. In a nation where young black males comprise less than three percent of the population and commit nearly half of all homicides and two-thirds of all violent crimes, mostly against each other, it's time for less rhetoric and some serious soul searching.

Brutality Against Illegal Immigrants Is Exaggerated

by John Corry

About the author: *John Corry is a senior correspondent for the* American Spectator, *a conservative monthly magazine.*

It was Rodney King all over again, with a reminder of O.J. Simpson. An 80-mile chase on California freeways in April 1996 ended when a truck carrying twenty-one illegal Mexican immigrants finally stopped. Videotape shot by a helicopter news crew caught two sheriff's deputies clubbing the driver of the truck and a passenger with nightsticks. The videotape was shown over and over on CNN, and it made all the evening news programs. Cries of outrage immediately followed. The Mexican government charged racism, while the White House expressed concern, and civil rights and immigration groups held demonstrations. Hypocrisy lay thick on the ground, along with intrusions into domestic politics. Republican rhetoric, apparently, had led to the beating of the Mexican driver and his passenger. Actually, they were lucky they only got clubbed.

The Provocations

Consider the provocations. The truck evaded a Border Patrol checkpoint. Various police units then pursued it, reportedly at speeds up to 100 miles an hour. Passengers in the truck threw beer cans at the pursuers. When the camper frame on the truck became loosened, they threw chunks of that. Meanwhile, the driver of the truck sideswiped cars, presumably as a diversionary tactic. When the truck stopped, the occupants bolted, except for the driver and two passengers. Two sheriff's deputies from Riverside County then approached, while the news crew hovered overhead. An international incident was born with the resulting fifteen seconds of videotape. It showed that the Mexicans offered no resistance when the deputies hit them. The driver of the truck, Enrique Nunez Flores, suffered a hairline fracture of an elbow. His companion and perhaps common-law wife, Alicia Soltero Vasquez (or Leticia Gonzalez, depending on which paper you read, and when you read it), required no immediate medical attention, although apparently she suffered bruises. It was unclear what happened to the other passenger—he wasn't on the videotape—although his lawyer said later that he also had been beaten.

Grant now that the deputies acted improperly. As the *Los Angeles Times* and virtually every other California news organization reported, they had violated Riverside Sheriff's Department guidelines. The *Times* noted that on the video-tape, "neither deputy can be seen discharging pepper spray, and neither appears to display his baton as a warning to the suspects before striking them." The *Times* also reported that one of the deputies "once was associated" with a group of deputies "who adopted a swaggering attitude to make it clear they would not tolerate lawbreakers." A few days later, the *Times* disclosed that the deputies had yelled first at the illegal immigrants in English and not Spanish. An audio tape made by the California Highway Patrol had revealed that the deputies shouted "Get down" at the driver and the two passengers. Then they hit them; only then did they say, *"Manos aqui"*—Spanish for "hands here."

Presumably, the two deputies will now be punished, although hopefully not because one was once associated with other deputies who swaggered, or because neither, at a time of high stress, spoke in English and not Spanish. On the other hand, you never know. Media coverage focused more on the big picture—incipient

> *"After leading the police on an 80-mile chase, ... [a captured illegal immigrant] may be thought fortunate to have suffered only a fractured elbow."*

racism, police brutality, immigrants' rights—than it did on the actual incident, and someone has to pay. Reporters and correspondents do not empathize with cops the way they once did. After leading the police on an 80-mile chase during which he sideswiped other vehicles, while his passengers threw beer cans, Enrique Nunez Flores may be thought fortunate to have suffered only a fractured elbow. The coverage, however, suggested otherwise.

The Unsympathetic Media

At the Radio-TV Correspondents dinner in March 1996, Marc Morano, Rush Limbaugh's man in Washington, asked Walter Cronkite to comment on CBS correspondent Bernard Goldberg's charge that the media had a liberal bias. "Everybody knows that there is a liberal, that there is a heavy liberal persuasion among correspondents," Cronkite replied. "Anybody who has to live with people, who covers police stations or covers county courts, brought up that way, has to have a degree of humanity that people who do not have that exposure don't have."

Cronkite, though, had it backwards. In the media age, correspondents do not cover police stations or county courts. They drop in only for the really big story, and miss almost everything else. Police stations and county courts deal with bad people who make good people miserable. If the correspondents hung around more, their humanity would be widened considerably, and they would be more sympathetic to all the rest of us, even to, or perhaps especially to, the police.

At the same time, some things simply had to be reported. In the same story in which it covered the beatings, the *New York Times* said that the Mexican Ministry of Foreign Relations had sent a stiff letter to the U.S. Department of State. The letter expressed "indignation" over the California incident and the "flagrant violation of the human rights of Mexican citizens."

> *"The United States treats Mexican illegals quite well."*

Three days later, in a story from Mexico City, the *Times* reported that Jose Angel Pescador, the Mexican consul in Los Angeles, was encouraging "at least four Mexican-American and Hispanic grassroots organizations in California" to take their protests to the streets. The *Times* also reported that the IPR, Mexico's long dominant political party, said in a statement that the beatings showed "how far racist and xenophobic attitudes have reached in the United States.". . .

Subsequently, the *Washington Post* ran a piece by veteran journalist Lou Cannon on an opinion page. It began with a sensible warning about relying on the videotape to determine what really happened; it concluded with a plea for an investigation into the "pattern of attitudes and policies toward illegal immigrants." As Cannon saw it, they "often have been depicted in political campaigns as alien invading hordes who are a menace to the United States.". . .

Truck driver Flores, openly encouraged by the Mexican government, filed a suit against Riverside County for more than $10 million, alleging that the deputies "recklessly, intentionally and wantonly beat him." The suit should be laughed out of court, but it won't be. Immigration disputes with Mexico get a free pass.

Illegal Immigrants Are Treated Well

No prominent news organization, columnist, or commentator seemed particularly upset when the Mexican consul in Los Angeles began calling for demonstrations. Surely someone should have demanded that he be deported. No one seemed upset, either, when the Mexican Foreign Ministry lodged its absurd complaint about the "flagrant violations of the human rights of Mexican citizens." Surely someone should have told the Foreign Ministry to go stuff it. The United States treats Mexican illegals quite well. A . . . story in the *Washington Times* reported on a survey of 456 Mexicans whom the U.S. had deported. The survey, taken by the newspapers *Reforma* and *El Norte,* found that 51 percent of the deportees said immigration officials had given them "good" treatment; 34 percent said the treatment had been "regular." Regular meant that someone had shouted at them or used disrespectful language. Only 13 percent said they had been treated poorly, and that figure was suspect. Only one deportee described a violent incident.

Moreover, if illegal Mexican immigrants are caught crossing the border with children, they are released in the United States and not returned to Mexico. They may then receive medical care, schooling for the children, and welfare benefits if they should have more babies. Mexico treats its own illegal immigrants quite differently. Joseph Perkins, a columnist for the *San Diego Union-Tribune,* calls this "the dirty little secret that the Mexican government tries to keep quiet." It rounds up illegal immigrants from Central and South America and deports them as quickly as it can, whether they have children or not. Meanwhile, the California beatings may have attracted enormous attention in both the United States and Mexico, but almost no attention was paid to a similar incident a few weeks later. Perkins wrote about that:

> After a 130-mile high-speed chase from southern Los Angeles County to Tijuana, Mexican police did not merely beat 16-year-old Elizabeth Asuna into submission. They shot the American teen in the back before taking her into custody. There was no "human chain" formed along the border to protest the girl's shooting. There were no indignant protests by high-ranking government officials in either Sacramento or Washington. There were no lawyers filing multimillion-dollar damage suits on Miss Asuna's behalf.

Perkins says there is a "double standard in U.S.-Mexico border policy." He is right, and he appears to be one of the few journalists who cares about it. There is a double standard in journalistic practice, too. The killing of seventeen farm workers by Mexican police at a rally near Acapulco in 1995 did not receive as much coverage as the California beatings. The press is most comfortable looking in only one direction.

Efforts to Reduce Police Brutality Should Not Interfere with Effective Crime Control

by George L. Kelling

About the author: *George L. Kelling, the coauthor of* Fixing Broken Windows: Restoring Order and Reducing Crime in Our Communities, *is a professor of criminal justice at Rutgers University in New Brunswick, New Jersey, a fellow of Harvard's Kennedy School of Government, and an adjunct fellow of the Manhattan Institute.*

The assault and torture of Abner Louima by New York City police officers in August 1997 was an abomination. It was an appallingly deviant act, not representative of the New York City Police Department, of policing generally or of good order-maintenance tactics. But critics of the police—from radical civil libertarians to political opportunists seeking an issue in the race to unseat popular GOP Mayor Rudolph Giuliani—are exploiting this disgraceful event in an effort to derail New York City's highly successful crime-prevention efforts.

Their outcry since the assault on Mr. Louima raises a couple of pressing questions: Did Mr. Giuliani and his former police commissioner, William Bratton, "unleash" the police to brutalize citizens? And are cities that are following New York's model—instituting policing policies based on the conception that disorder breeds crime—putting their citizens at risk from rampaging cops?

The stakes involved in answering such questions are high. The murder rate in New York has declined by 49% since 1993; other serious crimes are down almost as dramatically. While debate is raging about how to explain this spectacular success, few can doubt that police have played an important role. New Yorkers can only be grateful that thousands of people are alive; hundreds of thousands have not been victimized; and public spaces that once were out of

George L. Kelling, "The Assault on Effective Policing," *The Wall Street Journal*, August 26, 1997. Reprinted by permission of the author and *The Wall Street Journal*; ©1997 Dow Jones & Company, Inc. All rights reserved.

control are now available for children and families—all thanks in no small part to a revitalized police force and its effective order-maintenance policies. The virtual elimination of crime as a serious problem in the subway, for example, has no credible explanation aside from police action.

Powerful Ideologies

Yet it is precisely the policies that have produced these dramatic results that are now under attack. Lurking behind the dispute are powerful ideologies. The success of New York City, and of the many other cities that have established similar efforts to restore order, directly contradicts the ideology that has reigned in American criminology since the 1960s. According to the older view, poverty, racism and social injustice cause crime. To deal with crime, society must deal with its causes. Therefore, police can do little about crime except respond after it occurs and, perhaps, "displace" it—move it around a bit. This view further holds that the enforcement of laws against minor offenses merely serves to harass the poor, minorities and the homeless, limiting pluralism and diversity by imposing "middle-class" conceptions of propriety.

Police strategy nationwide until the late 1980s was largely consistent with this ideology. Police were "law enforcement officers" whose function was to arrest people after they commit serious crimes. So as not to be too intrusive, officers were sequestered in cars, isolated from citizens; they entered community life only in response to calls for service or when they observed serious offenses. "Victimless" crimes—prostitution, underage public drinking, aggressive panhandling—were effectively decriminalized.

> *"Yes, police abuse of minorities has been a problem and must stop; injustices should be corrected. . . . But crime control should not be held hostage to achieving these goals."*

The crack epidemic of the late 1980s made clear the dimensions of the urban disaster such policies had wrought. Levels of crime had been at unacceptable levels for more than two decades. So mean were the streets that when rapacious youths competed for control of public spaces to deal drugs, they had only to contend with each other: Public spaces had been largely "depoliced" as officers retreated into their cars. Police first, and prosecutors later, discovered that although they were unquestionably doing their job well, it made no difference. Despite vast numbers of arrests, vigorous prosecutions, and more and longer imprisonment, conditions on the street continued to deteriorate.

Restoring Order to the Streets

This paradigm began to change in the late 1980s. Police began to move out of their cars, interact with citizens and use existing legal authority to rein in outrageous and out-of-control youths. Local ordinances, nuisance-abatement procedures and housing and sanitation codes all became powerful tools as police restored order and began to retake public spaces. Police also rediscovered the potential of partnerships with other governmental agencies, neighborhood associations, business improvement districts and churches.

A resounding early success occurred in New York City's subway, whose police force Mr. Bratton headed in 1990 and 1991. In a matter of months, Mr. Bratton's new focus on disorder crimes like panhandling and turnstile jumping restored control; serious crime plummeted by 80%. The citywide story, begun when Messrs. Giuliani and Bratton took office in 1993, was a replay of the subway success. They linked disorder and crime, proving that police can make a difference and that crime prevention doesn't require radical social engineering.

> *"The pursuit of faultless policing should not be allowed to drive out good policing."*

Civil libertarians, who had successfully held crime control hostage to their social agenda for decades, have been fighting this shift of police strategy in virtually every U.S. city. In New York City, political and libertarian elites have agitated against "rampant" abuse, strip searches and handcuffing of "innocent" citizens. The rhetoric gets divisive and ugly. Former Mayor David Dinkins, for example, has hyperbolized: "Not since the heyday of the Klan have African-American men been at more serious risk."

The courts have been the civil libertarians' most potent weapon. Before the bench they regularly argue that police order maintenance infringes upon constitutionally protected free speech, equal protection and freedom of movement. To support their legal arguments they provide ample and unsupported propaganda: Police, they argue, conduct "wars" against the poor, minorities and the homeless; abuse of the poor and minorities abounds and is worsening; the "homeless" are society's victims, entitled to jobs, shelters and homes. Underlying it all is the big lie that disorderly behavior is victimless.

Judges are all too eager to join in the sophistry. The Florida Supreme Court asserted that police would not be able to distinguish between prostitutes hailing customers and housewives waving to their husbands. A federal district judge in California declared that sprawling in a stupor on a public sidewalk is a political statement, protected by the First Amendment. In New York City, a federal district court deemed unconstitutional a ban on subway panhandling. Although this ruling was later overturned by the Second U.S. Circuit Court of Appeals, the Second Circuit upheld another ruling, throwing out a citywide panhandling ban on similar grounds.

Such judgments betray an abysmal ignorance about the scams and hustles of urban street life. But what is most dismaying is the failure of judges to understand that the rhetoric about "war against the poor" and imposition of "middle-class mores" is phony—belied by every shred of empirical research. Northwestern University political scientist Wesley Skogan conducted research in 40 urban residential neighborhoods. He demonstrated that citizens of all social, racial and ethnic backgrounds agree on what constitutes disorder, intuitively link disorder with serious crime, and insist that police do something about it. Anyone who has talked seriously with inner-city residents understands their desperate desire for order and safety. Both Mr. Skogan's research and the subsequent experience in New York confirm that citizens are right and civil libertarians are tragically wrong: Disorder breeds serious crime.

Held Hostage

Yes, police abuse of minorities has been a problem and must stop; injustices should be corrected; and the genuinely needy should be helped. Each of these problems is important in its own right. But crime control should not be held hostage to achieving these goals, however worthy they are.

Done right, police order-maintenance activities grow out of a neighborhood consensus about what constitutes disorder. They honor the rule of law and bring citizens together by reducing their fear. The larger message of the Abner Louima horror is only that depraved individuals can lead any human endeavor astray. Police departments must recruit good citizens, train them well and provide them with guidance and leadership. Legislators and courts must give them good laws to enforce. Reasonable systems should be in place to identify abuse, corruption and deviance; when they occur, swift punishment should follow. But the pursuit of faultless policing should not be allowed to drive out good policing.

Media Reports of Police Brutality Are Incomplete

by Nancy L. Ford

About the author: Nancy L. Ford is the editor of Partners Off Duty, *a bimonthly newsletter for family and friends of police officers.*

I was a bridesmaid in my sister-in-law's wedding. My job was to walk down the aisle holding a single lighted candle. I did so graciously, smilingly, as did the other bridesmaids. The camera recorded this moment. It's hard to imagine, watching the videotape of my calm face that the entire time I was walking down the aisle, the scorching, dripping wax from the candle was burning me with every step I took.

Imagine if there were a camera taping a fight between you and your husband, only it didn't show the part where he came tromping into the house with his boots full of mud and grass clippings hanging from every stitch of clothes on his body. The camera also doesn't reveal the fact that you're to be entertaining a group of friends at your house in exactly 15 minutes. How would this look to you? Do you think that your anger would be perceived as overblown, unreasonable, unnecessary?

The True Rodney King Story

What if you were to watch a videotape, with no audio accompaniment, of a suspect being beaten by police in an attempt to control him. You would think, "That is totally unnecessary!! Look, he's complying with their orders! What's wrong with those cops?" Now take a listen to the background that you were unaware of and which should have been available to you in order for you to make a fair assessment.

The pursuit is a high-speed one on a usually crowded freeway. Then onto side streets. Narrow, run-down side streets with abandoned cars on both sides, potholes and debris. In the weeks preceding this pursuit, there had been a murder of a peace officer and threats of more to come as gangs sought fame in taking down an officer of the law.

Reprinted from Nancy L. Ford, "One Dimensional Judgments in a Three-Dimensional World," *LEAA Advocate*, Winter 1997, by permission of the LEAA.

The car is heading straight towards a park which is gated off; closed at night because of the heavy drug and illegal activity which occurs in the evening hours. Ambushes are commonplace in this terrifying world of law enforcement where one moment you're responding to a call, the next moment you're being shot at. This park is a hangout for gang members. It's dark. It's wooded. It's the perfect place for an ambush.

When the gated-off entrance is encountered by the car, the driver quickly exits the vehicle and refuses to cooperate. Approaching the officer, shaking his hips and affecting the crazed demeanor of an individual on illicit drugs, he shows no regard for his own safety or that of the officer. The officer draws her weapon; according to her training, the next and only recourse she has is to shoot the suspect. And she better hope she kills this hulk of a man who contemptuously mocks her; he's over 6' tall and weighs upwards of 300 lbs.

> *"We didn't smell the sweat, . . . hear the thud of a fellow officer being thrown to the ground, witness the wild-eyed behavior . . . coming from the suspect."*

Backup arrives. A different agency has taken control of the call. In an attempt to de-escalate the situation, the supervisor orders all guns be holstered. This has the intended effect on the suspect. He turns his attention to the newly arrived officers.

Still refusing commands, he charges one of the officers and bodily picks him up. He then throws him to the ground. The air is electric with the anticipation of the officers and the volatility of the suspect. Erratic and unpredictable behavior punctuate the dangerous prospects of their intended goal: gain control of the suspect and get him 'cuffed.

The rest, as they say, is history. The entire world was treated to innumerable viewings of a heavily edited and substantially shortened videotape. Judgments rendered, riots ensuing, societal exultation of the habitual offender who is the subject of all this chaos. Two officers in federal prison. Unprecedented attempts to lengthen their prison term. The criminal around whom this all centers violates the law again and again, with seeming impunity.

An Unqualified Judgment Call

Consider the facts above that we were unaware of, the reality of the situation we had no ability to grasp purely by virtue of our limited perspective—our armchairs. We didn't smell the sweat, feel the heat of an overworked engine, watch an officer draw down, hear the thud of a fellow officer being thrown to the ground, witness the wild-eyed behavior and the undecipherable language coming from the suspect.

Our stomachs weren't tightened by the anticipation of the moment. We weren't trying to control the suspect while keeping an eye out for any sympathetic gang-bangers who would be eager to lend a helping hand.

We made a judgment call we were unqualified to make. We viewed a one-dimensional image and made a three-dimensional supposition.

Whatever you think of the incident once you have the entire picture is up to you. The judgment we render while ignorant of the whole scope of any situation is up to us. Let's not be hasty.

The Media Overemphasize Police Brutality

by Joseph Sobran

About the author: *Joseph Sobran is a syndicated columnist.*

The alleged police torture of a Haitian immigrant in August 1997 has New York City in an uproar, complete with a protest march and the arrival of Johnnie Cochran to offer legal assistance to the victim.

Though some details are in dispute, nobody is defending what the police in the case are said to have done, for the simple reason that it was indefensible—and extremely repulsive. The Haitian, Abner Louima, had the handle of a toilet plunger shoved into his rectum and then into his mouth. His injuries were serious; so was his degradation.

The case was further inflamed by the racial angle. The cops are said to have used racial epithets while torturing him.

No wonder so many people are outraged. And no wonder Johnnie Cochran sees the case as an opportunity.

And yet worse police violence fails to stir similar outrage. If the police had shot Mr. Louima to death, the story might have passed quickly, with little local protest and no national media coverage.

The *Chinatown* Principle

Why? Think of it as the *Chinatown* principle. You may not remember many of the hundreds of movie murders you've seen, but you'll never forget the moment in *Chinatown* when Jack Nicholson gets his nostril slit with a switchblade. He requires only a few stitches, but an ingeniously nasty little injury can make far more impact on viewers than a thousand routine homicides.

Mr. Louima is by no means the most unfortunate victim of police criminality. But anyone hearing a graphic description of his experience is likely to be more sickened by it than by, say, the fatal shooting of a fleeing, unarmed 14-year-old shoplifter. We take fatal shootings for granted.

Likewise the racial angle could be insignificant. Mr. Louima's torturers may have used the racial epithet as a mere handy insult. But an ethnic insult can turn a single incident into a city-splitting cause celebre. It might have been different—no, it would certainly have been different—if the cops and the victim had been of the same race.

The *New York Post* gave two full pages of coverage on Aug. 29, 1997, to the Louima story, which is preoccupying Mayor Rudolph Giuliani and the City Council as well as much of the city's population. Further inside,

> *"An ingeniously nasty little injury can make far more impact on viewers than a thousand routine homicides."*

the same issue ran briefer stories under the headlines "Harlem Granny Slain in Apt." and "Boyfriend Held in Tot's Death." But despite their horror and pathos, these are conventional stories. They won't cause any uproar or lead to marches and protests. We take them for granted.

In the not-too-distant past, the details of Mr. Louima's torture would have been deemed too gross for publication in a newspaper. Now they are given in top-of-the-hour broadcast news reports. The degree of public reaction depends heavily on media standards of decorum.

Those standards are in constant flux and are never very consistent. In the quarter of a century since the Supreme Court struck down all the abortion laws of the 50 states, the major media have adopted a practice of avoiding graphic depictions of abortion. After tens of millions of abortions at every stage of pregnancy, few Americans know what it looks like. We have seen vivid atrocities televised from Somalia, Israel, Lebanon, Bosnia and Rwanda, but we have rarely seen "the termination of a pregnancy."

Arbitrary News Reporting

This raises interesting questions for the television age. Is the public being fully informed when it is merely told facts, without graphic details and, where possible, pictures? Is the news being slanted when the media use inflammatory details and pictures at their discretion? Are we entitled to see as well as to read and hear? Why are some facts shown in living color, while others are merely reported verbally?

Obviously the news media can't report, let alone show, everything that happens. To some extent their selection of story and detail is bound to be arbitrary, sometimes shaped by a sense of drama, by political preferences, by racial attitudes, or by simple humor.

But it's hard to avoid feeling that journalism, despite its serious pretensions, is now more akin to entertainment than to history. True, it's often grim entertainment. But so was *Chinatown*.

Chapter 2

What Factors Contribute to Police Brutality?

Chapter Preface

People across the nation were stunned by a particularly violent incident of police brutality in August 1997. Abner Louima, a Haitian immigrant, claimed he was beaten and sodomized with the handle of a toilet plunger by four New York City police officers, who then shoved the stick into his mouth, breaking several teeth. As with the videotaped beating of Rodney King by Los Angeles police officers six years earlier, Americans once more wondered how police officers could turn so brutally and so sadistically against the citizens they were charged with protecting.

Some officers and police experts blame police brutality on the "Blue Wall of Silence," an unspoken law enforcement code of conduct that forbids police officers to speak out against a fellow officer. This code of silence, according to critics, leads many police officers to believe that their fellow officers will defend their beating of a suspect or, at the very least, not report the brutality. Some observers contend that the police officers' code of silence extends outside the area of law enforcement as well. They argue that when people who are knowledgeable about a particular case of police brutality—such as health care workers who care for a beaten patient—and yet do not notify the officer's supervisor, it shows that they condone the officer's behavior.

However, others who study the police say the wall of silence is a myth. They claim that New York City police officers have testified against officers accused of brutality since 1857, when Officer Cairnes was arrested for shooting and killing Sailor Jack. Perhaps the most famous instance is that of Frank Serpico, who investigated corruption in the New York City police department in the 1970s. According to *New York Daily News* reporter Mike McAlary, who was the first to report Louima's torture, more and more police officers are speaking out against brutality; in fact, he asserts, it was a police officer who tipped him off about the story of the Louima beating.

Some experts on police behavior maintain that the "Blue Wall of Silence" is not the only reason police officers use excessive force to subdue suspects. Racism, challenging police authority, assertive policing policies, and inadequate training are also mentioned as possible causes. The authors of the following viewpoints examine these and other factors that are believed to contribute to police brutality.

Racism Causes Police Brutality

by Salim Muwakkil

About the author: *Salim Muwakkil writes on African-American issues for* In These Times, *a weekly socialist newsmagazine.*

Shortly after midnight on July 30, 1995, Joseph Gould was working as a "squeegee" on the streets of Chicago's trendy River North district. Gould, a homeless man, was dashing from car to car, washing the windshields of passing motorists when he encountered Gregory Becker and his girlfriend leaving an area nightclub. Becker, an off-duty Chicago cop, reportedly took offense at Gould's aggressive sales tactics and ultimately fired a 9-mm bullet through the homeless man's head, killing him. Becker—who is married and reportedly was anxious not to be found in the company of his girlfriend—quickly fled the scene and would likely have escaped detection were it not for alert witnesses who noted his license plate number.

Lenient Treatment

But the prosecutor and the judge dropped murder and manslaughter charges against Becker, citing conflicting witness accounts and insufficient evidence. The white, 35-year-old police officer was charged only with two counts of official misconduct for failure to report a shooting and for firing his weapon.

Becker's lenient treatment is this city's contribution to the unfolding national debate about police racism and corruption. Though police racism usually sparks little interest outside the black community, a string of astonishing stories have spurred a broad, if temporary, national debate on the subject. In August 1995, the nation was treated to the virulently racist remarks of Los Angeles Police Department Detective Mark Fuhrman, whose words were captured on audiotapes obtained by O.J. Simpson's defense team. And police departments in Philadelphia, New Orleans, New York City, Detroit, Cincinnati, Minneapolis and Washington have all been in the news regarding the behavior of their "bad apples."

Still, the Chicago story remains a particularly egregious study in how the sys-

Reprinted from Salim Muwakkil, "Cop Out," *In These Times*, October 2, 1995, by permission.

tem is structured to protect the misdeeds of its enforcers. "The Becker case is a perfect example of how the system is actually in collusion with corrupt police officers," says Patricia Hill, a 15-year Chicago cop and president of the city's African-American Police League (AAPL). "Just as the Los Angeles criminal justice system protected and promoted Fuhrman and the thousands of other Fuhrmans in its ranks, the system here immediately reacted to protect Becker. It's a cultural impulse on the part of white institutions."

Hill is part of a new breed of black police officers who are outspoken in their denunciation of racist actions and expressions both within police ranks and in the department's community relations. Her group, the AAPL, was founded in the late 1960s, and the militance of the era shaped its character. Members were routinely harassed by department brass, and it required a series of lawsuits by the group to force the adoption of mild affirmative action measures.

Because of varied affirmative action policies, many departments made modest gains in recruiting black cops during the 1970s and 1980s. Since 1972, the number of black police officers has doubled to more than 60,000. According to a report in the *Wall Street Journal,* the nation's 50 largest police departments increased the number of black officers by an average of 36 per cent between 1982 and 1992. But black cops still complain about biased treatment and increasing numbers are beginning to speak out against the system's structural racism.

Racist Assumptions

"We must remember that the very first police forces in this country were the slave patrols, so certain racist assumptions are designed into the very structure of policing in America," says William Geller, associate director of the Police Executive Research Forum, a Washington-based group that studies law enforcement issues. "Racism is prompted and exacerbated by the economic fears of whites, and police are seen as the thin blue line protecting them from their fears. That's the structural set-up that gets us in so much trouble."

Geller has authored and edited several books on the subject of police abuse of force, including *Police Leadership in America: Crisis and Opportunity.* Geller, a white researcher, is considered one of the most knowledgeable commentators on issues of policing. His recommendations echo those long heard in the black community. "Police must be more informed about, and culturally sensitized to, the communities they serve and lose that us-versus-them mentality," Geller argues. "Instead of

"Racism is pervasive in this police department and in just about every other one in this racist country."

being bad-guy chasers from the outside, police have to be intimately involved in helping to build more competent communities."

Philadelphia, a city that during the tenure of Police Chief Frank Rizzo epitomized the model of police-as-community-adversary, is once again gaining notoriety for its corrupt cops. So far six officers have pleaded guilty to charges of setting up innocent victims, tampering with evidence, selling drugs and brutalizing people, mostly poor black people in the city's 39th District. Consequently, 46 of their criminal convictions were overturned, and federal investigators have since expanded their search and subpoenaed logs of as many as 100,000 arrests over 10 years.

> *"Zero tolerance for racism from the top is the only way to eliminate the [racist police officers] within police departments."*

"All of the officers involved so far have been white and all of the victims black," explains Lesley Seymore, a veteran Philadelphia cop and the chair of the National Black Police Association (NBPA). "Despite the gross racial disparity, folks in Philadelphia say this is not an issue of race, just police corruption. Well, I respectfully disagree," she says. "Racism is pervasive in this police department and in just about every other one in this racist country. But in the departments there is a strict code of silence. And outside the department, the general society would rather deny this racism exists. All of this denial accounts for the fact that so little has changed in police culture. Mark Fuhrman was no aberration; neither was the beating of Rodney King. The only aberration was the technology that enabled other people to witness those routine occurrences."

Racist Behavior Condoned

But even after witnessing the savage mauling of King, a Simi Valley jury not only acquitted the officers involved, it condoned their behavior. And Becker, the off-duty Chicago cop, so far has escaped all but the mildest charges for killing Gould. A similar pattern is emerging in the wake of the Fuhrman tapes. Widely read *Chicago Tribune* columnist Mike Royko, for example, devoted a recent column to a reader's angry response to his earlier criticism of Fuhrman. Although Royko kept his distance from the reader's views, he provided a lengthy excerpt.

"I would challenge you and all the other hypocrites who are so quick to condemn Fuhrman to walk in some young cop's shoes for six months," Royko's respondent wrote. "You might find it hard to suppress the 'N-word' from your thoughts. . . . If it weren't for the Fuhrmans out there, our society could soon be another Rwanda or Botswana. There are a few of us—maybe more than you think—who realize this."

Royko's reader likely expresses the thoughts of many citizens, both white and black. The specter of criminal anarchy grows more ominous as the gap between rich and poor grows wider.

Clashes Between the Discontented and the Police

One of the predictable results of the economic restructuring that has slashed company payrolls and sent so many U.S. jobs overseas is a sharp rise in the ranks of the discontented. And, as Geller notes, it only follows that clashes between the most discontented and the forces of order also will increase. Thus Geller is not surprised by the recent proliferation of tales about police misconduct and racism.

Also unsurprised are members of the NBPA. At its national convention in Orlando in August 1995, the group was besieged by media people eager to know what effect the Fuhrman tapes would have on the NBPA's agenda. "I told them that the issues raised by the Fuhrman tapes are the reason we exist in the first place; it's always on our agenda," explains Ronald Hampton, the group's executive director.

Hampton spent 23 years on the Washington, D.C., police force and is convinced that zero tolerance for racism from the top is the only way to eliminate the Fuhrmans within police departments. "When an officer is found guilty of some manifestation of racism, fire him or her on the spot. If you can't work with the people who make up our communities, then you have no business being a police officer," Hampton says.

Community Policing

There is a consensus among critics of the prevailing police culture that the best chance for reform lies in the widespread adoption of "community policing" strategies, which require officers to work more closely with local residents. "We need to broaden the training," says Hampton. "We need to alter our reactive policing strategy and completely transform our policies to work in closer concert with the community." Hill of Chicago's AAPL argues that current policing techniques are completely inappropriate. She even proposes that police be renamed. "If we called ourselves 'Domestic Peace Officers' it would help reorient our thinking. We must become community citizens, not protectors of the white supremacist status quo."

Many veteran officers dismiss the community policing concept as an inappropriate, "bleeding-heart" strategy dreamed up by effete sociologists. Despite this attitude, arguments

"This country's widening social divisions increasingly place police on the firing line."

in favor of the concept are slowly penetrating the calcified ranks of department brass. Variations of the concept are being implemented in numerous cities, and it appears that it may be the policing trend of the future. But the change will be hard-fought.

"I've seen some small changes in the Philadelphia Police Department," notes the NBPA's Seymore, "but even the tiniest change required tons of effort. Our efforts within the various departments will only be successful if we get political support and encouragement from the community."

Perhaps the public outcry following the Fuhrman tapes will help generate support for efforts to uproot racism and corruption within police departments.

But judging by past experience, these efforts will likely be short-lived. Following the videotapes of the Rodney King beating, for instance, the high-profile Christopher Commission was empaneled to investigate and suggest reforms for the LAPD. The commission found numerous problems and made many recommendations—few of which have been implemented.

As Geller notes, this country's widening social divisions increasingly place police on the firing line. And unless a strong social movement suddenly arises—one that demands economic reforms as well as police accountability—we are on track for more trouble between police and those they allegedly serve and protect.

Police Often Overreact to Challenges to Their Authority

by Deborah Sontag and Dan Barry

About the authors: *Deborah Sontag and Dan Barry are staff reporters for the* New York Times.

After dropping her young daughter with a baby sitter, Taquana Harris rushed to her hostess job at the fashionable Bowery Bar one night in February 1997, her leopard-print evening gown sweeping elegantly through the dark, icy streets of the East Village. Then a strange woman crudely grabbed her by the arm and demanded to know what she had done with the drugs.

Within seconds, Ms. Harris recalled, she found herself pinned to the steel grating of a bodega by two plainclothes officers engaged in a neighborhood drug sweep. Frustrated by the officers' refusal to hear her explanation for being on that particular block, Ms. Harris made a tactical mistake: she wisecracked. "Oh, I get it," she said. "You're trying to reach a quota."

The Heart of the Issue

One officer responded with pepper spray, blasting her in the face. Distraught and weeping, Ms. Harris was taken in handcuffs to the Ninth Precinct station house, where she was charged with disorderly conduct and resisting arrest. Later that night, months before the charges were dropped and the city paid $50,000 to settle her claim of civil rights violations, one of the arresting officers left her with some parting words: "You don't talk to police officers the way that you did."

The officer's comment, in an otherwise mundane case, drives to the heart of what links Ms. Harris's unsettling encounter to the worst cases of police brutality. However they end, be it with a strip search or a face slammed into the pavement, most misconduct cases begin with what the officers perceive as a challenge to their authority.

Such challenges lie at the root of so many civil rights lawsuits, and of so many academic studies of police behavior, that they are recognized as a phenomenon unto themselves. They provide the catalytic moment when, with the hint of power shifting from an officer to a citizen, routine encounters can escalate into explosive incidents. One officer may feel challenged by taunts, another by the simple question, "What did I do?"

These challenges continually test the relationship between civilians and the police, who are given guns, nightsticks and wide latitude to keep order. In New York City, that tenuous contract is tested even further by the

> *"Most misconduct cases begin with what the officers perceive as a challenge to their authority."*

often brash assertiveness of the city's residents. More so than elsewhere, experts say, the New York police are called on to show unnatural restraint in their dealings with the public.

The New York Police Academy tailors standard police training to instruct new officers on how to absorb verbal aggressiveness like a sponge, or, in the martial arts language they use, to "bend like the reed in the wind."

The Reeds Are Not So Supple

Once planted on the real streets of New York, however, the reeds are not so supple. Many officers see disrespect as a threat, not just to their job performance, but sometimes to their lives. For them, choosing to dominate testy citizens without overasserting themselves is not only an art but an attitude. Some situations, they believe, require forcefulness, and there is a fine line between appropriate and inappropriate force.

Officer Michael F. Wilson, a 13-year veteran of the force who teaches sociology at the Police Academy, said many officers struggle to rise above their visceral reactions to disrespect.

"Initially, when someone gives you major grief, you're stunned," he said. "It's like the first time you got punched as a kid. You're shocked, and your body wants to react. In the best of cases, though, there is this little person inside your head saying, 'It's not worth it. I put my hands on this person, I lose.'"

Spokesmen for the police argue that the thousands of police misconduct claims a year in New York City should be put in statistical context. Every year, the department makes 330,000 arrests and issues 1.5 million summonses for moving violations, and the great majority of those encounters are handled properly.

But critics say the recurrence of garden-variety misconduct cases like that of Ms. Harris's reflects the failure of the Police Department to alter something deeply embedded in the police culture: an us-versus-them mentality that makes many officers distrustful of those they encounter on the street. And they point out that, as the police aggressively enforce Mayor Rudolph W. Giuliani's "quality of life" strategy, the number of misconduct and excessive force claims has increased significantly from 3,956 in 1993 to 5,596 in 1996.

An examination of dozens of police misconduct cases suggests that a variety of challenges to police authority—asking for a badge number, videotaping officers, leading them on a chase—can provoke an incident. Some officers feel irritated when someone files a complaint against them, others when a bystander intervenes in their handling of an encounter.

The officers' responses also vary, from the proper, nonconfrontational handling of a matter to a vindictive arrest, from a thwock with a flashlight to a debilitating beating.

Brutal Encounters

One young man, Douglas Snyder, a New York University student, was kicked in the face until he lost consciousness after videotaping a police confrontation with squatters; the camera was smashed and urinated on. Another, Edward Dominguez, a high school student in the Bronx, was a passenger in a speeding car; an officer kicked him so hard in the groin that he lost a testicle.

In such encounters, the person usually ends up charged with one or more of what civil rights lawyers refer to as the triumvirate of charges: resisting arrest, disorderly conduct and the obstruction of governmental administration. Those charges are almost invariably dropped, but not before punishment has been delivered in the form of a humiliating strip search or a night spent in a holding pen.

> *"Many officers see disrespect as a threat, not just to their job performance, but sometimes to their lives."*

In addition to traumatizing some law-abiding citizens, experts say, these cases cost the city millions of dollars in lawsuits and immeasurable capital in public trust.

"I used to be the kind of person, when I see an officer, I smile," said Nancy Tong, a documentary filmmaker who was taken into custody for speaking disrespectfully to an officer. "I'm not that kind of person anymore."

New York's most notorious recent cases of police brutality stem from what the officers saw as challenges to their authority.

Prosecutors say that an officer's mistaken belief that Abner Louima was behaving aggressively toward him prompted the beating he gave the Haitian immigrant inside a Brooklyn station house. Francis X. Livoti, the officer dismissed in 1997 for using a choke hold that led to the death of a Bronx man named Anthony Baez, explained that he moved to arrest Mr. Baez and his brother because, he said, they refused to stop playing football when ordered, "daring" him to "take some kind of action."

"Like Livoti, many officers experience rampant disrespect and view it as undermining their authority," said Stuart London, a lawyer who won Mr. Livoti an acquittal on murder charges and represents many officers accused of misconduct.

"Every day," Mr. London said, "throughout the city, you have officers who are routinely turning the other cheek. But sometimes they feel they have to take a stand in order to patrol effectively, and then something minor can really escalate."

Ill-Chosen Words

It was a hot August night in 1994 when Ms. Tong, the filmmaker, was caught in bumper-to-bumper traffic on the narrow streets of Chinatown, and, she said in an interview, climbed from her car to peer at what lay ahead.

From behind her, a voice barked, "Get back in that car!"

Ms. Tong, 43, an immigrant from Hong Kong, shot back: "What's the big deal? It's a free country." When she turned around, she drew in her breath. She had unwittingly talked back to a police officer.

She ducked back into her car and when traffic began to move, the officer ordered her to pull over and demanded her license, which she had left at home. She asked what she had done. The officer got very angry, she said, and told her driving was a privilege, not a right. He then told her the computer showed her license was suspended, which it was not, as he later admitted. Ordering her out of the car, he handcuffed her and took her into custody.

At the Sixth Precinct station house, she was strip-searched in a bathroom by a rubber-gloved matron, who took away her belt and keys. She was locked in a holding cell until the early hours of the next morning, then released with two tickets: one for driving without a license, the other for "failure to comply with an order." Both were later dismissed, and Ms. Tong sued the city.

"Unfortunately for them, I know a little bit about my rights," she said. "This is not China." She won a $35,000 settlement in 1996.

Ms. Tong's case typifies a pattern in which the blunt and often abrasive language of New York City aggravates an encounter with the police. Police experts say that the city's officers and residents expect one another to withstand a little verbal abuse. But some police officers perceive sarcasm and insult as direct challenges to their authority and, experts say, overreact.

"New Yorkers have big mouths," said Paul Chevigny, a law professor at New York University and an expert on police culture. "More of them are on the liberal side, and are more critical of authority, than in other places.

"A variety of challenges to police authority—asking for a badge number, videotaping officers, leading them on a chase—can provoke an incident."

"In a way, I find New Yorkers charmingly naïve. They imagine they live in a city where they can challenge authority and not get hurt. They're wrong, and that's too bad."

Officer Wilson, the Police Academy instructor, said he urges young officers not to take things personally. "I tell them people are not mouthing off at you,

Mike Wilson, but at the uniform, the authority," he said.

A challenge to police authority does not have to be verbal. In several cases examined, people had their tape recorders or video cameras damaged or their tapes taken, suggesting that to record some officers at work is to provoke them.

> *"Some police officers perceive sarcasm and insult as direct challenges to their authority and, experts say, overreact."*

During the city's celebration of the Fourth of July in 1995, some squatters reclaimed an East Village tenement from which they had been forcibly removed by the police several weeks earlier, then trumpeted their small victory by hurling bricks and firecrackers at the police. The department responded by sending hundreds of officers to the building, including dozens in riot gear.

Across the street, several college students had gathered on a rooftop to admire the fireworks over the East River, but turned to watching the struggle below. At one point, some police officers clambered up to the roof to question them, court records show, but left after being satisfied that the students were not involved in the fracas.

But Douglas Snyder, a New York University photography student, later said that he began to videotape the confrontation after seeing officers strike pedestrians with nightsticks and shields, just as the lights of a police helicopter above washed over him.

Minutes later, Mr. Snyder testified during a deposition in 1997, several police officers in riot gear stormed the roof with guns drawn. The officers screamed for everyone to "get down," several witnesses testified, then began kicking the students. Two officers ran over to Mr. Snyder and smashed his recorder, he said. Then one kicked him in the face until he lost consciousness.

Megan Doyle, Mr. Snyder's girlfriend at the time, began to scream. She later testified that officers threw her to the ground and put a gun to her head, calling her "slut" and "whore." Then she, Mr. Snyder and several other students were handcuffed, arrested and held for several hours on charges of disorderly conduct.

The morning after the encounter, Mr. Snyder found his smashed camera on the roof. The tape was missing.

The charges were dropped several weeks later, and in 1997 the city paid $50,000 to Ms. Doyle and $42,500 to Mr. Snyder to settle their lawsuits.

Power to Arrest Can Be Abused

Dr. James O'Keefe, the director of training at the Police Academy, says the academy works to instill in officers a wary respect for the public, and to convey the lesson that emotion should never overtake reason.

For decades, the academy operated like a boot camp, in which verbal abuse was thought to prepare recruits for the streets. But officials came to suspect that the approach also taught officers to treat citizens in a similarly harsh manner.

Chapter 2

After a phase using transactional analysis, an approach based on a form of popular psychotherapy, the academy now uses the martial arts paradigm to convey the importance of bending like a reed. In classes and role-playing situations, officers are taught that verbal attacks don't threaten them, and that their role in a confrontation is to end it, not win it.

But those officers who respond inappropriately to challenges have more at their disposal than flashlights and batons to exact punishment. Officer Wilson spells out to recruits why they always have the upper hand. "At the end of the day," he tells them, "you have the power of arrest."

In most police misconduct cases, civil rights lawyers said, that power seems to be abused. In such cases, officers often level charges to punish someone who has shown them disrespect, or to cover up their mishandling of an encounter, the lawyers said.

In Los Angeles, Merrick Bobb, a special counsel to the city, tracks the use of such charges as resisting arrest or disorderly conduct, noting when they are leveled and dropped, as one way to identify problem officers.

"You find clearly that often those contempt-of-cop arrests are filed by the police officer as a way to cover a use of force that may be questionable," Mr. Bobb said. "You also find that these charges get dropped because they are not valid."

New York City does no such tracking, although the police misconduct files suggest a similar pattern.

The case of Sahar Sarid is one example. Manhattan prosecutors declined to prosecute Mr. Sarid, 22, for resisting arrest after an encounter with the police that landed him in a hospital emergency room earlier this year. His mistake, he said, was responding to a request for his license and registration with a question, "Why?"

A month after emigrating from Israel, Mr. Sarid became confused by Manhattan traffic patterns and unknowingly drove the wrong way down East 62d Street before being stopped by the police on York Avenue. When he questioned the order to produce his license, an officer punched him in the arm, he said. He was directed to pull over in a bus stop, he said, only to get a ticket later for illegally parking there.

Mr. Sarid then climbed out of his car, he said, and refused to get back in, telling the officers he feared getting struck again. That, he said, pushed the officers to kick his legs

> *"In most police misconduct cases . . . [the power of arrest] seems to be abused."*

out from under him, beat him with their fists, handcuff him and twist his fingers. "Go back to the Middle East," he said he was told.

On the way to the station house, the arresting officer warned Mr. Sarid not to bleed all over his cruiser, and then punched him again, he said. Terrified, he began to hyperventilate, and was taken to New York Hospital instead. Hospital records show that he was treated for a bloody nose and abrasions on the cheek and forehead.

Mr. Sarid sought the assistance of Dov Hikind, a Brooklyn Assemblyman who helped him find a lawyer. A strong supporter of the police, Mr. Hikind scoffed at the idea that Mr. Sarid had done anything wrong. "This is one of the most abusive cases I've ever seen," he said. "If this guy resisted arrest, why did they drop the charges?"

Hell on Wheels

Among the most provocative ways to challenge police authority, as Rodney G. King learned, is to engage officers in a car chase. As Jerome H. Skolnick and James J. Fyfe noted in *Above the Law* (The Free Press, 1993), their study of police conduct, "Fleeing motorists become prime candidates for painful lessons at the end of police nightsticks."

Edward Dominguez, 17, and his brother-in-law, Vicente Fernandez, then 20, did not consider themselves to be fleeing motorists on a spring night in 1993, just speeding drivers traveling a deserted highway at 70 miles an hour. Mr. Fernandez, a Dominican immigrant who works in his father's supermarket, had just picked up Mr. Dominguez, an American-born Dominican, from his job at one of his father's Mexican restaurants in the Bronx.

The men remember making a U-turn on Gun Hill Road, but said they were unaware at the time that a police cruiser began following them after the illegal maneuver. During testimony in a Police Department trial, however, the officers said they were forced to chase the young men at high speed on the Bronx River Parkway until Mr. Fernandez's car broke down.

> *"Among the most provocative ways to challenge police authority . . . is to engage officers in a car chase."*

With guns drawn, two officers pulled the two young men from the car, threw them on the ground and handcuffed them, both sides said. Mr. Fernandez was struck twice in the head with a police revolver, which left him with a bump on his forehead and a cut on the back of his head, according to hospital records.

With both men face down on the ground, Officer Francisco Rodriguez repeatedly asked where they had stolen the car, ignoring Mr. Fernandez's claim that it was his mother's. When Mr. Dominguez asked what they had done wrong, he said, the officer told him to shut up and spread his legs.

Then, Mr. Dominguez said, the officer kicked him hard in the groin, causing excruciating pain. One testicle swelled so much that weeks later it had to be removed.

At the police station house, a nauseated Mr. Dominguez told Sgt. Henry Pelayo that he was in pain from an officer's abuse. The sergeant, Mr. Dominguez said, told him no one had harmed him. When the young man insisted, according to prosecutors, the sergeant placed his hand on his gun and said: "No, you fell! Nobody hit you. You fell."

About 3 A.M., the young men were released to Mr. Dominguez's father, who drove them to the hospital. Mr. Dominguez's sister called the Civilian Complaint Review Board and filed a complaint. By dawn, the incident was under investigation, and the young men were interviewed by the police as they sat in wheelchairs in the emergency room.

Plausible and Corroborated

A year and a half later, during the officers' departmental trial, Rae Downes Koshetz, the Deputy Commissioner in Charge of Trials, found the young men's complaints about their injuries at the hands of the officers to be "plausible, promptly made, unexplained by the respondents, and corroborated by independent medical evidence."

She found Officer Rodriguez guilty of physical abuse and of calling Mr. Fernandez a "Dominican faggot." Referring to the "gratuitous nature of the misconduct and the serious injury inflicted on Dominguez," she recommended that he lose 30 days' pay and be placed on probation for a year.

She found Sergeant Pelayo guilty of bullying and threatening the men, of "misconduct per se" and of condoning the misconduct committed at the scene. She recommended suspension without pay for 20 days, which Commissioner William J. Bratton upgraded to a 30-day suspension. . . .

Mr. Dominguez, meanwhile, dropped out of high school in his senior year, had a psychological breakdown and, at 21, is supported by his father. He was briefly married, but the marriage ended because he was unable to father a child due to his injury, he said.

He was born and raised in New York, but is considering moving to the Dominican Republic for a fresh start.

Assertive Policing Contributes to Police Brutality

by Dennis Cauchon

About the author: *Dennis Cauchon is a staff reporter for* USA Today *newspaper.*

Jose Sierra Jr. points to a scar on his forehead. A cop from the 70th Precinct put it there in 1994, he says. Sierra was drinking a beer and playing dominoes with his buddies in front of Jimenez Spanish Grocery in the Flatbush section of Brooklyn, New York, when the cop told him not to drink in public.

One word led to another, and Sierra found himself in the back of a police car having a police radio smashed into his face.

"'Go ahead, file a complaint, you low-life Puerto Rican,'" he says the cop told him. "'Every time we see you, we'll f--- with you.'"

Sierra filed a complaint, he says, but authorities, when asked about his case, declined to look for the information. According to the American Civil Liberties Union (ACLU) of New York, only 1% of the citizen complaints lodged since July 1993 against New York City police officers resulted in any disciplinary action.

But these days, complaints like Sierra's are getting more attention, particularly in the 70th Precinct, now that police officers have been accused of nearly killing Haitian immigrant Abner Louima on August 9, 1997, by sodomizing him with a toilet plunger in the station house bathroom. Louima's bladder and colon were torn. . . .

Assertive Policing

The case, which has resulted in criminal charges against four officers in the precinct, also has stirred a debate about the New York Police Department's strategy of "assertive policing."

"Assertive policing," an aggressive variant of what's often called community policing, has been credited with sharply reducing crime throughout the city. It is being copied in Washington, Houston, St. Louis and other cities.

Mayor Rudy Giuliani has dubbed his city's version "zero tolerance," because it means enforcing every law, no matter how minor, from jaywalking to playing loud music.

Louima was originally charged with disorderly conduct, for tussling with police officers who were trying to quiet a disturbance at a Brooklyn nightclub. Giuliani later ordered the charge dropped.

The theory behind assertive policing comes from sociologists James Q. Wilson and George Kelling, who argued in a 1982 article in the *Atlantic* magazine, "Broken Windows," that paying attention to seemingly small things—broken windows, graffiti—creates a sense of order and lawfulness that reduces overall crime and improves a community's quality of life.

Retaking Streets

The 70th Precinct has embraced assertive policing. The cops have gotten out of their patrol cars and started walking the streets. The precinct's force has increased from 210 to 330 since 1991. Now, if you're drinking beer on the sidewalk, you're going to pour it out. If you're playing your boombox too loud, you're going to turn it down. And some residents say assertive policing means that if you talk back to a cop here, you're going to get busted, perhaps even beaten.

Using assertive policing, the officers of the Seven-Oh, as the precinct is called, have taken back the streets of Flatbush for law-abiding citizens. The rate of serious crimes such as murder, rape and robbery has dropped 51% since 1993 in the precinct.

But having a more aggressive police force also creates more opportunities for confrontations between officers and civilians.

"When you tell the cops to go after every little problem and defend them in knee-jerk fashion no matter what the accusation, as Giuliani has until this case, you create an anything-goes attitude on the police force," says Norman Siegel, head of the ACLU of New York.

Giuliani, a former prosecutor, and his top aides have said there is no connection between assertive policing and allegations of police brutality. "Pro-active policing doesn't mean the police officers have a license to be abusive," says Lenny Alcivar, director of press operations for the police department.

> *"Having a more aggressive police force also creates more opportunities for confrontations between officers and civilians."*

Since the Louima case, the mayor has ordered every officer in the city to join discussion groups with the department's critics so that they will understand the concerns of civil liberties groups and minority leaders. He has also appointed a

28-member task force that will spend $15 million investigating police brutality.

Former New York police commissioner William Bratton, who resigned in 1996, denies that brutality is an unofficial or inevitable part of assertive policing. He blames the youth and inexperience of individual officers, saying brutality complaints went up after the hiring wave of the early 1990s boosted the New York force from 25,000 to 38,000. Once the new officers get more experience and the bad ones wash out, complaints will drop, he says.

> *"An increasing number [of brutality complaints] come from people who were neither arrested nor given a ticket, an indication that they arise from assertive policing."*

New York cops' biggest problem is their mouths, according to Bratton. "They've always got to have the last word," Bratton says in frustration. He notes that most complaints are for verbal attacks, not physical ones. "You're hiring kids these days who use the f-word as every other word. Then you tell them, 'As a cop, you can't use that word,'" Bratton says.

New York officers have been reluctant to speak on the record since the beating. Four who agreed to speak privately said the attack on Louima was a criminal act. Three of them added, however, that it was crucial to an officer to be perceived as a physically tough person on the street.

Mix of Good and Bad

The Seven-Oh Precinct isn't New York's toughest. The Bronx has precincts with higher crime rates. But it's a big, busy, dangerous precinct nonetheless, 3 miles long and a mile wide, home to 160,000 people from myriad cultures.

The Brooklyn Dodgers used to play at Ebbets Field here. Now, Flatbush is a place where the Wonderland Day Care Center's sign is written in English and the Cyrillic letters of Russian. It is home to both Orthodox Jews and the mosque of Shiek Omar Abdel Rahman, the blind cleric blamed for the World Trade Center bombing in 1993.

The largely white police force watches over the mostly minority residents from a cavernous police station built of stone and brick on a Flatbush side street in 1909.

A lot happens here.

In 1993, in the same bathroom where the recent beating is alleged to have occurred, a drug suspect grabbed a cop's revolver and pumped four bullets into two cops, who survived. The suspect died from a point-blank gunshot to the forehead. The official finding was that he turned the gun on himself.

In 1994, a uniformed officer was photographed at the station wearing a Ku Klux Klan hood. The officer said he was clowning around.

The typical Seven-Oh cop is about 30 and white, and commutes from outside New York City. Seven-Oh cops have nicknamed themselves "The Laws of Flatbush," a reference to *The Lords of Flatbush*, a movie about a gang of toughs who roam Brooklyn streets.

Many residents feel profoundly grateful to "The Laws of Flatbush" for what they've done to make the neighborhood a safer place. They recount stories of great courage and kindness on the part of individual officers who know the neighborhood closely, a principle of assertive policing.

Nancy DiCoscia, who runs the Looking Great Beauty Salon, says that when a customer was mugged near the shop, an officer not only responded quickly but offered the victim some money. "We said, 'No, we will take care of it,'" says DiCoscia. The officer came by the next week to ask how the mugging victim was. "They are very good people," she says.

Haitian immigrant Raymond Arias says a Seven-Oh cop saved his 4-year-old cousin's life. The boy had fallen from a fourth-floor fire escape. An officer arrived immediately and rushed the child to the hospital without waiting for an ambulance. But Arias tells stories, too, of overly aggressive police treatment.

In 1995, he joined 15 other Haitian college students to protest the political situation in Haiti. The cops called the protesters "idiots." The protesters yelled that they were better educated than the cops. The students took out their college ID cards and held them high.

"As soon as we did that, oh boy, we were in trouble," says Arias, now 29. The cops swarmed the protesters and arrested them. Arias says that on the way to the station, a Haitian was beaten with a heavy object wrapped in a towel to prevent wounds from showing.

A Trend Indicated

Official records show that although complaints against police officers are lower than they were at their peak in 1985, they climbed in the 1990s and reached 5,596 in 1996.

Citizen complaints are an imprecise measure of police brutality. Some citizens, including Sierra, say that filing a complaint with the Civilian Complaint Review Board is useless, because so few complaints—about 1%—are found to be valid. Sierra says his complaint went nowhere, that he wasn't even interviewed.

A spokesman for the board, Sherman Jackson, said he had no information on Sierra's complaint but that 50% of the people who file never show up when summoned for a face-to-face interview.

But the complaints point to an important trend: An increasing number come from people who were neither arrested nor given a ticket, an indication that they arise from assertive policing. And in cases where the race of the complainant is known, 80% were black or Latino, according to former mayor David Dinkins.

Police Attitudes Contribute to Police Brutality

by Jerome H. Skolnick and James J. Fyfe

About the authors: *Jerome H. Skolnick is a law professor at the University of California in Berkeley. James J. Fyfe is a professor of criminal justice at Temple University in Philadelphia and a former New York City police officer. They are the authors of* Above the Law: Police and the Excessive Use of Force.

How can police, who can be exemplary heroes, beat people and then be prepared to lie about it?

Policing, because it is a 24-hour-a-day identity, generates powerfully distinctive ways of looking at the world, cognitive and behavioral responses that, when taken together, may constitute "a working personality." How working cops learn to see the world around them, and their place in it, offers a key to understanding their motives, fears and aspirations, as well as the moral codes by which they judge themselves and affect the lives of others.

A Sense of Mission

People who are attracted to policing do not see themselves as bullies, nor does the literature on policing suggest they are authoritarian personalities. Rather, they tend to be upright, virtuous and civic-minded. The typical police recruit is white, physically fit and agile, of the lower-middle or working class, male, in his 20s and with some college education.

Robert Reiner, a leading British police scholar, has contended that a sense of mission is a central feature of the culture of police. "This is the feeling that policing is not just a job, but a way of life with a worthwhile purpose, at least in principle." Oddly enough, it may be precisely this sense of mission, this sense of being a "thin blue line" pitted against an unruly and dangerous underclass that can account for the most shocking abuses of police power.

Yet where wide disparities in culture, social class, geography and affluence separate people at the top from those at the bottom, the disadvantaged are virtually certain to view the police as oppressive representatives of the group that is keeping them down. Thus, especially when race is a ready marker for differences of advantage, it is extremely difficult for police who work in inner-city slums to overcome the distrust and resentment of the people who most need good police service. Where police departments make no effort to overcome those barriers or, worse, where they fail even to acknowledge that they exist and cling instead to some simplistic version of "color-blind professionalism," latent resentments become open antagonism. It is hypocritical for police who work in cities where social class and race make so much difference in everybody's life to claim that they can perform their work uninfluenced by such considerations.

> *"It may be precisely this sense . . . of being a 'thin blue line' pitted against an unruly and dangerous underclass that can account for the most shocking abuses of police power."*

Complaints about police conduct most often arise when cops encounter people who may not be engaging in criminal activity but whose conduct suggests that they might be, or might be the sort of people who would if they could. A police manual cautions cops to attend to "suspicious persons known to the officer from previous arrests, field interrogations and observations"; "persons who loiter about places where children play"; "known trouble-makers near large gatherings"; and "cars with mismatched hubcaps."

As a necessity and a consequence of maintaining their high state of readiness, police develop a perceptual shorthand for certain kinds of people as "symbolic assailants"—persons whose gestures, language or attire the police have come to identify as being potentially threatening or dangerous. This sort of apprehension and sensitivity tends to isolate police, an isolation that may be pronounced when they are patrolling in vehicles. Even before community and problem-oriented policing became acceptable, the 1967 Civil Disorder Commission advised officers to get out of their cars, into the neighborhoods and on the same beat or assignment long enough to know the people and the neighborhood's prevailing conditions.

Categorizing the Citizens

But even when police know the people and neighborhoods, they must distinguish the known from the unknown or unfamiliar. John Van Maanen, who studied police in a place he called "Union City," developed a tripartite typology to categorize how police viewed the citizens with whom they came into contact.

Suspicious persons, the first category of Van Maanen's typology, are those who seem incongruous in their surroundings. When police stopped such persons, they usually treated them in a brisk, professional manner.

Police have developed all sorts of strategies for legally extracting information from citizens. Once a stop is made, an officer can ask to search the car. The driver, usually confused as to "rights," rarely refuses. Cops know this; they learn how to manipulate such encounters to appear forceful. They later testify that the person "volunteered" to be searched when it was clearly in their self-interest not to be.

Paradoxically, people in the "overclass" may be especially prone to respond politely to an officer's request for information. They fit the description of what Van Maanen calls "know-nothings"—citizens who know nothing of the world police inhabit. They are the citizens for whose benefit police will present a courteous and efficient performance.

Most learn early to respect the authority of a police officer and that it is impolitic to challenge that authority. When he or she does, especially when he does, he may find himself occupying Van Maanen's third and most evocative category, that of "the ---hole"—a person who denies, resists or questions police authority.

Paul Chevigny similarly explains the origins of much police brutality in "Police Power," his extensive two-year study of police abuses in New York City during the 1960s. Chevigny identified "the one truly iron and inflexible rule": "Any person who defies the police risks the imposition of legal sanctions, commencing with a summons, on up to the use of firearms."

A Three-Step Process

Chevigny described a three-step process leading to excessive force. Step 1 is a perception by police of a challenge to their authority. The "wise guy" is thought by the officer to be presenting himself as superior to the cop. In Step 2, when police have so defined the malefactor, an arrest, according to Chevigny, would almost invariably follow.

Whether it did or not depended on the offender's response (Step 3). If the citizen admitted being a wise guy, or turned polite and complied with the officer's request, he was usually released. If he persisted in defying authority, an arrest would typically follow. If he further persisted, he would be taught a lesson of compliance by being beaten, then charged with resisting arrest, in addition to the original charge.

> *"We should routinely videotape police conduct during those occasions where propensities to excessive force are most likely to occur."*

Albert Reiss Jr., who with Donald Black conducted a systematic study of police coercion for the President's Commission on Law Enforcement and Administration of Justice, reported that, of the incidents of excessive force recorded by observers, nearly half occurred when the victims verbally defied police authority. The authority that was defied was not "official" but the personal authority of the individual officer. "Often he seems threatened," Reiss observed, "by a simple refusal to acquiesce to his own authority. A policeman beat a handcuffed offender because, when told to sit, the offender did not sit down."

Chevigny was sensitive in his three-step paradigm to two other considerations. First, an ordinary citizen begins to assume the status of a pariah only when actively defying the police, while an outcast group member may be presumed to be a potential offender. Consequently, when such a person is arrested, the arrest can be considered the ethical, if not the legal, equivalent of arresting a criminal. The arrest can be justified on grounds that even if the outcast has not committed a crime this time, he has been guilty many times in the past.

Second, Chevigny notes that it also may be more difficult for members of minority groups to show the submissive qualities middle-class people learn to use when dealing with authorities. The words "Sorry, officer" often feel like galling words of submission to the downtrodden and are especially hard for African-Americans to say. "The combination of being an outcast (Step 1)," he writes, "and refusing to comply in Step 3 is explosive; thereby hangs the tale of many police brutality cases."

Routinely Tape the Police

To the degree possible, we should routinely videotape police conduct during those occasions where propensities to excessive force are most likely to occur: high-speed chases, interrogations, protests and riots. But the videotape is only a technical tool deriving from a larger principle of police reform, which is that anything we can do to reduce the insularity of police is a good thing. A clearer definition of what police can and cannot be expected to accomplish will reduce officers' tendencies to use excessive force of the kind the public was exposed to in the beating of Rodney G. King in 1991. Over the long run, this can only enrich the work of line cops, more clearly define good policing, and help to see that we get it.

Police Culture Causes Police Brutality

by *Chicago Citizen*

About the author: Chicago Citizen *is a part of the largest black-owned chain of weekly newspapers in the Midwest.*

A representative of the U.S. Civil Rights Commission recently declared that police brutality is rampant in St. Petersburg, Florida, the site of two rebellions in 1996 over the issue of police murder.

In Pittsburgh, Pennsylvania, the Mayor has agreed to enter into a consent decree with the Justice Department to institute sweeping reforms to address patterns of police abuse which have plagued the Black citizens of that city for decades. The Mayor's willingness to take such an action is no doubt a direct result of the anger, outrage and massive mobilization/protests among community people over the police murder of Jonny Gammage. Police brutality, murder and misconduct are so prevalent in New York City that Amnesty International, a highly credible human rights organization, essentially labeled the "Big Apple" the capital of police brutality in the U.S. in a report issued in 1996.

Complaints About Police Brutality

All across the country more and more people are complaining about police brutality and misconduct. Though the loudest outcry about police brutality is emanating from the Black community and communities of color, complaints from White people are on the increase. Montel Williams aired a show on police brutality where some of the most vociferous critics of the police were White victims of police brutality. And, though it is White cops who are disproportionately involved in perpetrating acts of police brutality, unfortunately Black officers and officers of color have occasionally been found to be among the most brutal within police forces across the country.

During an interview on Bob Law's *Night Talk*, I asked Ron Hampton, executive director of the National Black Police Association (NBPA), for his analysis of what it is that breeds police brutality among police authorities in this nation.

Reprinted from the March 27, 1997, editorial of the *Chicago Citizen*, "Police 'Culture' Breeds Brutality and Misconduct," by permission of the *Chicago Citizen*.

Ron responded that there is a "police culture" and "mentality" which is responsible for the renegade cops who are terrorizing our communities. He noted that large numbers of people, particularly men, aspire to be cops precisely because they see it as an opportunity to exercise authority and control over people. A badge and a gun are also an outlet for many men to express their "machoness." Hence instead of becoming police officers to serve, protect and be accountable to the people in the community, far too many people become cops so that they can be "enforcers" of the law.

An Esprit de Corps

Hampton suggests that these negative motivations for joining the men and women in blue are reenforced in police academies where a kind of "we-against-them" attitude is cultivated intentionally or unintentionally. The community, particularly Black communities and communities of color, are seen as dangerous, crime-infested places which must be controlled. Police academies also consciously develop an esprit de corps that bonds the officers into a fraternity of sorts in which there is a strong sense of loyalty to one another.

"There is a 'police culture' and 'mentality' which is responsible for the renegade cops who are terrorizing our communities."

It is this esprit de corps which produces the infamous "blue wall of silence" which often shields officers who commit acts of police brutality and misconduct and prevents them from being prosecuted. As a consequence, while the community is well aware of the reality of police brutality and misconduct, it is extremely difficult to prove it because of the almost impenetrable wall of silence which serves as a protective cover for renegade cops.

Guilty of Complicity

While the majority of cops may be decent people who do not engage in acts of brutality and misconduct, they are nonetheless guilty of complicity with brutality and misconduct because their sense of fraternity and loyalty predisposes them to look the other way or be silent when renegade cops carry out their foul deeds.

At the 1997 National Emergency Conference on Police Brutality and Misconduct, a key issue for discussion will be how to root out renegade cops and how to make the police accountable to the community. Ron Hampton believes that there must be a major effort inside police departments to transform the culture that breeds police brutality and misconduct and that this process must begin with the training.

Chapter 3

How Does Police Brutality Affect Society?

Chapter Preface

The police department in New Haven, Connecticut, had a well-deserved reputation for police brutality and corruption during the 1980s. As is true of many police departments across the country, New Haven's police chief unfailingly supported his officers against charges of police brutality. Some say that this toleration for police brutality encouraged police officers to use excessive force when questioning and arresting suspects. When Nicholas Pastore became New Haven's chief of police in 1990, he made many changes to the department, including the withdrawal of automatic support to police officers accused of using excessive force.

Critics of Pastore's new policy concerning police brutality believe that it caused the crime rate to rise. They maintain that since incidents of police brutality were no longer tolerated by their supervisors, police officers became reluctant to involve themselves in situations that could turn violent. One police officer asked, "Why am I going to risk my butt to get into that situation when I know that even if I handle it well, I may face a departmental inquiry?" Pastore's critics assert that criminals became so emboldened by the new policy that they began to sell drugs openly on street corners in full view of New Haven's police.

Others believe, however, that brutality by New Haven police officers was responsible for much of the violence in the city. By preventing police brutality, they argue, other types of violence can be averted. According to New Haven's Child Study Center, "When police officers are in fact thoughtless or inconsiderate to a child in the course of their response to a crisis, they reinforce the child's experience of society as uncaring, and strengthen the child's belief that hostile behavior is the normative mode of adult functioning." Pastore himself attributes the rise in the crime rate to the easy availability of guns. The gun, he asserts, "makes us all less effective, and sometimes impotent."

The debate over New Haven's police brutality policy reveals that the use of excessive force has wide-ranging consequences. Police brutality affects not only the officer involved, the victim of the beating, and those who witness the incident, but society as a whole. It also changes the way society and its individual members regard the police. The authors of the following viewpoints examine some of society's responses to police brutality.

Police Brutality Reveals the Injustice of Capitalism

by George Kane

About the author: *George Kane is a staff reporter for the* New Unionist, *a monthly socialist newspaper.*

It is a common failing to believe that nothing ever changes. So with thinking about the police: we've always had them and we always will.

A Recent Institution

Actually, as chronicled by Jerome Skolnick and James Fyfe in their book, *Above the Law,* police forces are a relatively recent institution, a creation of the Industrial Age. In this country, police were introduced in Boston in 1837, and in New York City in 1845.

The early American police forces were modeled after the London Metropolitan Police, organized by Sir Robert Peel in 1829 after 50 years of recurring riots in the city. The transformation of English society brought about by the Industrial Revolution had created a propertyless class of wage laborers who could not vote. Mass protests were the typical means for the industrial working class to put forward their grievances, and mass protests frequently turned into riots. Also, high unemployment and chronic poverty caused a rise in crime coincident with the rise of industrial capitalism.

Social unrest reached a peak in the economic depression that followed the Napoleonic Wars. In 1819, a peaceful protest against high wheat tariffs in St. Peters field outside London fumed into a massacre when the army moved in to disperse the crowd. Eleven unarmed protesters were killed and hundreds wounded in an attack so shocking that critics called for a new government.

Public hostility against the army grew so great over the next decade that a new agency was needed for enforcing social order.

When Prime Minister Peel formed the police, he intentionally distinguished them as sharply as possible from the army. Soldiers wore red coats and carried rifles, so he dressed the police in blue and armed them with batons. Peel's at-

Reprinted from George Kane, "Police Brutality Part of 'Normal' Job of Cops in Protecting Rich Against Poor," *New Unionist*, November 1995, by permission of the author.

tention to public opinion was foreign to the insulated and often arrogant officers of the army, and has been instructive to every police administration since. Peel taught that the police could only succeed when they had the approval of the great majority of the populace.

In the United States, as in England, the need for police was seen when the social disruption caused by the industrialization of the economy became evident. Rioting frequently broke out between ethnic groups in competition for factory jobs. In the

> *"The Los Angeles police boast that every confrontation with a civilian must be a win for the police. They punish everyone who questions their authority."*

large cities in the Northeast, hostility between African Americans and Irish led to the most infamous race riots.

Following the successful English model, Boston introduced municipal police in 1837 to quell persistent social disorder. They have been ever since the omnipresent guarantor that the will of the government is enforced.

Government controls the behavior of its citizens in many ways, from taxation, licensing, loans, registration for the military draft and the threat of legal charges and court proceedings which may lead to loss of property or freedom. But of all departments of government, the police have a unique tool for enforcing the government's will. That tool is violence.

The nature of the violence depends on how willingly the citizenry accedes to the demands government imposes. If all citizens view the acts of the government as necessary and just, there is no need for violence to enforce the government's decisions. But when the demands upon a group of people are seen as unjust and intolerable, they can be enforced only through naked violence.

In a capitalist society, as in other forms of society that are divided into competing economic classes, the government cannot represent the interests of all citizens simultaneously. Since some groups in society will always feel government is acting against their best interests, the need for violent enforcement of the laws will always to some degree be present.

In class-divided society, government always ends up under the control of the most powerful economic class. In capitalist society, that class is the owners of the industrial wealth of production, distribution and finance—the owners of *capital*. In the United States, the government is dominated by this capitalist class through the two major parties. Police departments exist to defend the property of capitalists; to enforce the will of capitalists; to perpetuate the political and economic dominance of capitalists.

A Different View

However, most media and academic "experts" have an entirely different view of the police. They assert that crime is everyone's problem, not only business owners'. After all, the victims of crime come disproportionately from the working class. Whether the crime is murder, assault, mugging or burglary, you are at greater risk if you are poor rather than rich, black rather than white, a resident of an urban ghetto rather than a gated suburban enclave.

By this reasoning, if the police reduce crime they will serve the working class much more than the privileged bourgeoisie.

The supporters of the police also dispute that their role is to enforce class rule by asserting that America is a political democracy. The government is not elected by the capitalists but by all the people. They contend that, as guarantors of the will of the government, the police are the guarantors of the will of the majority.

This view denies any role of the police in class conflict other than as neutral referees who see to it that both sides abide by the rules. For capitalist rule to endure, the majority of citizens must accept this benign view of the role of the police.

To test these two views of the police—hired goons of the ruling class or heroic protectors of the innocent and helpless—we have to look at the actual practices of police forces. Fortunately, this is easy to do. Many recent incidents have wiped away the thin veneer of police respectability and revealed for all to see a culture of arrogance and of contempt, both for law and for the public.

The Police's Function

First, let us distinguish between the police's function of responding to crime and their function of preserving social order.

In the latter function, in which the police are called upon to prevent and end riots, the class nature of the police function is immediately evident. Has there been any civil disturbance in which the police acted to protect people? Their function instead is to punish people—summarily, brutally and unforgettably.

I attended the University of California at Berkeley from 1967 through 1970, during which time I saw and was involved in more riots than I can remember. Always, they began as peaceful gatherings. Each time, a peaceful political meeting turned into a riot only when the police moved in. The only act of violence that I ever witnessed before the po-

> *"The police's role of holding society together through violence will become increasingly abhorrent and untenable."*

lice started swinging clubs was the breaking of one window.

Even when the police did not choose to precipitate a riot, they were never neutral referees of public order. Their role was to suppress social dissent.

In one anti-war demonstration that I did not attend, demonstrators were attacked by Hell's Angels hoodlums wielding heavy chains. The police stood by and did nothing.

This has been a recurrent tactic in crowd control, especially in racial rioting.

In violence between Irish and blacks in New York City in the nineteenth century, the police not only defended the white mob, they arrested blacks exclusively and often joined in beating blacks. In violence accompanying labor strikes, the police only arrest the strikers and do not interfere with the excesses of private security guards.

The pretense of class neutrality in crime control is also refuted by the reality of police practice.

The authority of the police is legitimized by the widespread belief that they perform their duties within the law, respecting the rights of criminal suspects. Yet, the newspapers are full of stories of police brutality, racism, vigilantism and falsification of evidence. In Philadelphia, falsification of evidence has been found to be so egregious that hundreds of convictions may be overturned.

A Pattern of Lawlessness

The pattern of police lawlessness has been documented in numerous studies, such as the Christopher Report on the Los Angeles Police Department after the Rodney King beating, and the Walker Report after the Chicago police riot in 1968. The *Los Angeles Times* ran an award-winning exposé of Los Angeles police misconduct in the early 1990s. In Minneapolis, the weekly *City Pages* ran an impressively researched report in 1994 on the brutality of the 10 officers who have cost the city nearly $5 million in civil judgments.

These reports expose a police culture of arrogance, confrontation, intimidation, casual contempt for the law and brutality. The pattern is so consistent that it cannot be dismissed as the work of a few loose cannons. Loose cannons would soon be driven off the force if they did not have the support of their colleagues. Instead, they protect each other with a code of silence that prevents most investigations of police conduct.

Frequently, police speak openly about their culture. The Los Angeles police boast that every confrontation with a civilian must be a win for the police. They punish everyone who questions their authority.

Low Credibility

Police credibility has sunk especially low among African Americans, who have been the object of police racism and a particular focus of the war on drugs. Two terms that have been indelibly etched in the relations between blacks and police are "occupying army" and "railroading."

A statistic released in 1995 is that an incredible one-third of all black males between the ages of 20 and 29 are currently under the authority of the judicial system, either in prison, on probation or on parole.

Police abuse is now so widely acknowledged that police authority has been delegitimized for much of the nation. The jury in the O.J. Simpson trial rejected the prosecution case in its entirety when they became convinced that racist cops planted the evidence. With that verdict, we have conclusively stepped past the era when police testimony is automatically accepted.

If the myth of police honesty and fairness continues to erode, capitalist rule itself will be rejected.

The delegitimizing of the police can be forestalled in the short-run by reforms such as civilian review boards over police conduct. But as the contradictions of capitalism impoverish the working-class majority, the police's role of holding society together through violence will become increasingly abhorrent and untenable. The people will be forced in self-defense to overturn capitalism itself.

Police Brutality Reveals Society's Racism

by Joseph C. Kennedy

About the author: *Joseph C. Kennedy holds a Ph.D. in social psychology from Columbia University. He works in African development.*

I have two sons. They attended public and private schools in New York and Washington, studied abroad in London, Rome, and West Africa, and graduated from a highly respected college in the Midwest of the United States. They never caused any trouble at school, at home, or in the streets. They were never on drugs, never involved in rape or carjackings. They "grew up right." Yet both have been arrested, jailed, and criminally charged, and we have heard the words "five to ten years mandatory" and "one to five years minimum."

My sons are black. And their experience has made clear to at least one black family that no black American—regardless of education, profession, wealth, or values—can be shielded from the capriciousness of racism. While Americans were divided over the O.J. Simpson verdict, most were appalled by the Mark Fuhrman tapes and their revelations of racism, manipulation of evidence, and perjury by a member of the Los Angeles Police Department. It would be easy and comforting to believe that Mark Fuhrman's behavior was an aberration, or that such racial biases and behavior toward blacks exist only in large city police departments like Los Angeles or Philadelphia. But as long as racism exists in American society, it will be found even among those sworn to uphold the law—in police departments and in criminal justice systems, in large cities and small towns alike.

I grew up in a small town in southern Ohio where there were few blacks. When I sat with my classmates in a restaurant after school, it was the police who would tell me to get out: "You are not wanted here." At the movies, it was the white policeman who told me to leave my seat and go sit in the back "where Negroes sit." In Texas, it was the white police who beat my brother and me on the head because we spoke of rights for blacks. It was the white police in Arlington, Va., and the District of Columbia who often followed my car, then pulled me over for no reason. So I did not consider the police my friends or protectors. Still, I wasn't prepared for what happened to my sons.

A "Black Man with a Beard"

In about 1985, the phone rang in my downtown Washington, D.C., office. It was my older son, then 30. "Dad! Guess where I am? I'm at the Arlington County Jail. Some woman told the police she had been robbed by a 'black man with a beard.' She picked my picture out of some pictures. You can get me out with a $500 bond." I posted the money.

My son and I embraced when he was brought out. Although his voice had been calm and matter of fact on the phone, I could see the disbelief and fear in his eyes. I could not disguise the same in mine.

A young policeman told us that my son was charged with the attempted robbery at knifepoint of a white woman at about 8:30 on Wednesday morning at an office building in Ballston. The officer paused, then said, "That's mandatory five to ten years. It will help that he turned himself in."

Turned himself in! What was he talking about? The afternoon before, Sunday, a detective with the Arlington County Police Department called asking for our son. I told him he was out but would call back. When I gave my son the message, we both thought it had to do with a pledge card he had filled out to contribute to the Arlington County Fraternal Order of Police, or with the Arlington Yellow Cab he drove when he wasn't working on his music and video production. Monday morning, on his way to pick up his cab, he stopped by the Arlington County Courthouse. When he met the detective, he was immediately charged and arrested.

> *"As long as racism exists in American society, it will be found even among those sworn to uphold the law."*

About a week earlier, while driving his cab in Arlington, a policeman had given him a ticket for a traffic violation. The police must have been on the lookout for a "black man with a beard." My son fit that description, so the police who gave him the traffic ticket must have phoned in his cab number to the criminal division, which then got his picture from his registered Hack-Taxi license.

My son had to establish where he had been on that Wednesday morning about two weeks earlier. For most people who have regular jobs, the answer would be rather simple, but when my son was not driving the taxi, he generally worked at home, alone. If he were at home on that morning, how could he prove it?

The Taxi Manifest

Fortunately, the roster at the Arlington Yellow Cab office showed he had taken out a cab that day starting around 6:00 a.m. As a radio-cab company, drivers respond to calls from a dispatcher who provides the name and address of the passenger to be picked up. If we could get the manifest, maybe it would show where he was that day at 8:30 in the morning.

That afternoon, my son called with jubilation. The manifest showed he had responded to a call at 8:15 in South Arlington. Destination: The Department of Agriculture Building on Independence Avenue in the District. The round trip would take at least a half hour. He could not have been in Ballston between 8:15 and 8:45, and indeed he had not been in the Ballston area that day. My son added that he had given this information to the detective who had arrested him. I didn't express it, but my joy turned to anger and fear. I didn't trust the police.

We found a lawyer who agreed to take the case for $1,200. When we mentioned the manifest, á la Perry Mason I fully expected the lawyer to talk with the arresting county officer and have the case dropped. Instead, he indicated there was nothing he could do; I suspected he thought my son was guilty. So using the manifest as a guide, my son and I went to the passenger's house. She remembered my son because they had talked about music. She willingly wrote a statement saying that on that specific day, she had been picked up at about 8:15 and dropped off at the Department of Agriculture on Independence Avenue.

Several weeks later, we went to court. Our lawyer approached us and told us that the woman who had filed the complaint wasn't going to show up and that the case had been dropped. Just like that, it was over. But it never should have begun. Would an arrest have been made with the simple description "a white man with a beard"? What would have happened if there had been a trial and my son had not driven his taxi that day? Odds are he would have been added to the statistics of young blacks in prison.

Round Two

In 1991, at about 1:30 a.m. on a Sunday morning, I was awakened by a shout from my older son: "Dad! Dad!" I immediately ran to the wide-open front door, where I was shocked by a cacophony of sounds and a blur of sights—the flashing lights of Arlington County Police cars, a patrol wagon, the crackling sounds of police radios, and seemingly dozens of policemen in my front yard and on the road.

Stepping out into the yard, I saw my older son with his video camera. Nearby, a black policewoman with her gun drawn was yelling, "I'm saying stay back. If you get any closer, I'll arrest you for obstruction. Do you understand me?"

I heard my younger son, who was 30 years old, cry out, "What have I done? What have I done?" Off to the left I saw our old green Granada in

"The police must have been on the lookout for a 'black man with a beard.'"

the driveway, and my son's friend standing on the far side of the car. Then I saw my son—spread-eagled and face down on the hood of a police car. Walking past the drawn gun, I saw he was handcuffed. He was crying again—"What have I done? Why are you arresting me? There must be a reason." My older son, my wife, and I called out, "What has he done? What is the problem?" The only response was, "Get back, get back or you will be arrested." It was chaotic. When my son cried out in pain, "Oh God, please get off me, I'm not doing anything," one policeman punched him in the side, then the other shook him and pushed him further into the hood of the car.

> *"Would an arrest have been made with the simple description 'a white man with a beard'?"*

I called out, "That's my son, let him up. We live here. Why are you arresting him?" The response: "You are bordering on obstruction of justice. We'll arrest you." One of two policemen who had been standing off somewhat detached said, "Let him up for a second. If you want to know what is going on, ask the arresting officer." Several times we called out, "Who is the arresting officer?" Finally a cocky voice answered, "I am making the arrest. Go put some pants on." (When my son had awakened me, in my haste I had run outside in my nightshirt.)

"Don't worry about my pants," I said. "That's my son, you are standing in my yard; before you put him in that patrol wagon, tell me what the charge is."

"If you want any information, call my supervisor. If you want to make a formal complaint come to the county jail. They'll be charged when they get to the station."

As they put my son, along with his friend who was also handcuffed, into the patrol wagon, I could see his face and jacket were covered with mud. At the County Detention Center, after a half hour wait at three in the morning, the magistrate appeared. "Your son was charged with assault and battery on a police officer, and his friend with obstruction of justice." After collecting $1,000 bond for each, he hung up his "Out to lunch" sign and disappeared.

The arresting officer came out. His uniform was clean, his face unmarked. In the same cocky voice, he remarked, "I didn't recognize you with your pants on." Our son came out. The left side of his face was swollen and covered with dirt, his eye nearly closed. His heavy jacket was ripped and covered with mud. So were his trousers.

We immediately went to the hospital. "He's pretty well beaten up," the emergency room attendant remarked. After about an hour of examination, the doctor released my son. His face and eyes were swollen, he had bruised ribs, and there were cuts on his wrists from the too-tight handcuffs. The doctor recommended he see a psychiatrist.

Good Citizens

When we left the hospital, the sun was coming up. My son, his friend, my other son, my wife and I drove home in silence, lost in thought. How could this have happened? Our son had always been kind, gentle, and courteous. He had been brought up with values of right and wrong, of obeying and upholding the law. He had never been in trouble. Over the past months he and his friend had been working extremely hard, and one of his TV productions would be airing soon. Yet he had been beaten in his own driveway. As a family, we had lived in Arlington for 17 years, paid taxes, voted, took pride in our neighborhood, contributed to civic affairs, including the Fraternal Order of Police. We were good citizens. But we were black. It all hurt. Whatever illusions of security from racism and injustice that may have remained since our first son's arrest were totally shattered. It hurt even more that my son—bewildered, handcuffed, in pain—had yelled out to me for help. I had always tried to be there for him, but this time I could not help him.

Over the next few months, we got caught up in a criminal system that seemed characterized more by racism and vindictiveness than by a regard for right and wrong, truth, and justice. Despite the dictum "Innocent until proven guilty," my son had to prove he was not guilty.

The Incident

We went to a highly recommended lawyer, part of a large, white, Washington-based firm. Our son explained what had happened. He and his friend had stopped at a popular all-night diner on Columbia Pike in Arlington. Sometime after 1 a.m., they left and drove leisurely in the old family 1975 Granada the 20 or so blocks along Columbia Pike, up the short hill, and then down the short steep hill which led to the family home—the last house on a dead-end street.

Unknown to them, shortly after they left the diner, an Arlington County Police car had started following them at a distance with its lights off. Halfway down the hill—about five seconds from the house—they were startled by the flashing lights of a police car. They pulled into the driveway and stepped out. A few seconds later a white policeman, flashlight in hand, bounded from the police car which had pulled up alongside the yard. My son called out "Officer, what seems to be the problem? Can I help you?"

"Get back in the car."

"Officer, what seems to be the problem? I live here. This is my house. May I help you?"

"Whatever illusions of security from racism and injustice that may have remained since our first son's arrest were totally shattered."

In a high, agitated voice the officer yelled—"Get back in the car." My son's friend got back in on the passenger side. As my son opened the door to get back in, the policeman, who was now standing in the driveway at the back of the car, called out "Come back here." My son knew there had been problems with the rear tail lights, but they had been fixed a few days earlier.

Remembering being stopped by white police officers on several other occasions in Arlington, on the New Jersey Turnpike, and in California—once at gunpoint—he walked slowly to the end of the car. He deliberately held his arms away from the sides of his jacket so there could be no mistake about his reaching for anything.

When he reached the end of the car, without a word the policeman suddenly grabbed for his right wrist. As my son pulled his arms away, the officer hit him with a vicious blow to the head, knocking him to the ground. He then grabbed his jacket collar and dragged him across the driveway to the opposite side of the car, kicking him in the side several times along the way. When the policeman saw that my son's friend had gotten out of the car, he yelled, "Get back in the car or I'll bust your head too." The policeman then kicked him a few more times, twisted his right arm, forced him face down into the wet leaves and rocks, and handcuffed him.

> *"We got caught up in a criminal system that seemed characterized more by racism and vindictiveness than by a regard for right and wrong, truth, and justice."*

Shortly afterwards, another patrol car arrived with a white male officer and a black female officer. They grabbed my son and threw him on the hood of the car. Other police cars and a patrol wagon arrived. When my son cried out that they were hurting him, one of the officers punched and pushed him. His friend, who was once again standing alongside the car, called out, "Why are you doing that?" The black female officer yelled, "Shut up. You are obstructing justice and resisting arrest," and handcuffed him.

The Police Version

At the police station they were told what the charges were. My son was asked to sign some papers. When he declined, the police said, "That's all right, we'll sign them for you." The police officer reported that he had followed the car because the tail light was out. He had tried to radio in the license number, which would have given the registered address of the vehicle, but his radio wasn't working.

As the car descended the hill, he turned on his overhead lights, but the car did not stop. Realizing that he had entered a dead-end street, his radio now working, he called for backup. The officer said that the driver had refused to get back in the car, had walked toward him in a menacing manner with his hands near the pockets of his bulky jacket, and without provocation, struck him. In self-defense, the officer was subduing him when another car with two officers arrived.

As our lawyer began discussions with the Commonwealth attorney's office, the true nature of the system began to unfold. The Commonwealth office suggested my son plead guilty—a suspended sentence would be recommended.

The next suggestion was to enter a plea of no contest—not admitting guilt but recognizing there probably was enough evidence to secure a guilty charge. Again, a suspended sentence would be recommended, but there could be no civil suit afterwards.

To Win at Any Cost

The Commonwealth was dismayed that we turned down their suggestions and that we were prepared to proceed to trial. Their determination to win at any cost soon became evident. Several days before the trial our lawyers learned that the Commonwealth attorney was going to present a motion to the District Court judge to have the case heard directly before a jury instead of the usual first step of a hearing before a judge. Their argument was that the case had received too much publicity. In fact, on the advice of our lawyers, we had deliberately avoided any publicity, even though we had been approached by the District and Arlington press and the National Association for the Advancement of Colored People (NAACP). But a number of our friends were incensed and had written the Virginia senators, the governor, and the Arlington County Board of Supervisors.

> *"The officer . . . admitted that he had followed their car . . . because there were two black males . . . in a predominantly white . . . neighborhood."*

If found guilty before a judge, my son would get a second chance before a jury, but if his first hearing was before a jury, he would have no second chance. The Commonwealth attorney's office undoubtedly believed its chances of a conviction were much better with a jury selected from the Eastern District of Virginia—which would more likely believe a black man had assaulted a police officer than that a black man had been beaten by that policeman—than with a judge. The assistant Commonwealth attorney—the prosecutor in the case—also bragged to one of our lawyers that "the judge always sides with the prosecution" in deciding on a judge or jury hearing. Even our lawyers were convinced that the judge would probably accept the motion and we would go before a jury later.

Trial by Error

The judge called the case at 10:00 on a Thursday morning, nearly two months after the beating and arrest. The assistant Commonwealth attorney confidently explained to the judge that since the case had received publicity and because people were interested—letters had been written to the county board and high officials—the case should be heard by the people, a jury, rather than before a judge.

Our lawyer countered by stating that one of the most cherished rights of the Constitution is that of free speech, of speaking out when there is a belief that an injustice has taken place—and furthermore he had full confidence in the judge's right and ability to hear the case.

The prosecuting attorney apparently did not realize she was actually questioning the judge's competence to rule on a case which had received "publicity." The judge ruled the case would be heard in her court that very afternoon. The assistant Commonwealth attorney, the Commonwealth prosecutors, and the three police officers were visibly shaken by the decision. For us, there was a ray of hope.

> *"The training materials used at the police academy were filled with racial and ethnic stereotypes."*

That afternoon the judge asked all of those who were to testify for the defense to leave the courtroom—our older son, my wife, myself, and my son's friend (whose charge had been dropped). He was alone with his lawyers. We waited outside the courtroom. As the minutes turned into hours, our tensions and anxieties mounted.

After about three hours, our son came bounding out of the courtroom with a huge radiant smile—perhaps the most radiant smile I have ever seen. The judge had thrown the case out, saying, "The police must be held to a higher standard than I have heard here today."

The arresting officer who had brought the assault charges had been the first witness. With precision, persistence, and extraordinary skill our lawyer caught him in inconsistencies and lies. Finally, the officer totally unraveled, broke down, all arrogance gone, and admitted that he had followed their car for nearly 20 blocks with his lights off, not because the tail light was out, but because there were two black males in an old car early in the morning in a predominantly white Arlington neighborhood. He had not attempted to use his radio to check on the license. When the car turned off Columbia Pike, went up the short hill, and suddenly turned onto a dead-end street, he turned on his flashing lights and radioed for backup. When two black men, both larger than him, stepped out of the car on that dead-end street bordered by woods, he panicked. He called the driver to the back of the car and grabbed for his arm. When the driver pulled his arm back he hit him, knocked him down, dragged him across the driveway through the mud, kicked him in the chest and ribs several times, and then handcuffed him. There had been no struggle.

Corroborating Lies

The white male officer who had appeared on the scene with the black female officer was the second witness. Not knowing the first officer had admitted everything, he took the stand and repeated his story—he and his partner had arrived in time to witness the "struggle" and handcuffing. At that point, without calling the black female officer, the judge threw the case out.

By accident, the mother of my son's friend, who had sat in the courtroom throughout the proceedings, walked into the large room where the assistant Commonwealth prosecutor, other Commonwealth prosecutors, and the three police officers were standing and sitting. With shock, bitterness, and anger, they were lamenting, "What went wrong? How did we lose? How could the judge do that?" They were consumed not with serving justice, but with winning.

The police officers who were sworn to uphold the law had lied and filed false reports. The officers had lied to the Commonwealth attorney. (Even more disturbing, maybe they had not lied and there had been a cover-up. An investigation by the department's internal review arm had found no cause to question the officers' reports.) They had lied on the stand. Their lies or the cover-up could have sent my son to prison. But justice had prevailed, thanks to a lawyer who believed in "innocent until proven guilty" and a judge who was concerned with the truth.

Pursuing the civil suit we filed was almost as nightmarish as what had come before. In deposition, the arresting officer admitted that similar charges of police brutality against blacks had been brought against him, but no official records existed because every few years the police records are expunged—the slate wiped clean. When it was discovered that the training materials used at the police academy were filled with racial and ethnic stereotypes (which meant the police were being trained to respond to stereotypes rather than to reality), the county attorneys worked mightily to prevent these materials coming before a jury.

> *"The anger that my sons faced prison terms simply because of their skin color, cannot be forgotten."*

The county's most effective tactic, however, was "financial exhaustion"—prolonging the pre-trial proceedings as long as possible with the knowledge that our personal finances would run out before those of the county. Ironically, we were fighting against ourselves because our tax dollars were supporting the county system.

In the end, the system won. Our lawyers advised us to accept a financial settlement as well as an agreement that the police academy would revise any racially stereotypical training materials. We settled because we knew the proceedings could go on indefinitely. The county could wear us down financially. We could go before a jury drawn from the Eastern Virginia District, and although the police admitted guilt, the jury could be unsympathetic to a young black and award us nothing. If they did award us something, the judge could decide to reduce the amount. Why spend more money and time and take that chance?

While numerous brutality complaints had been filed in Arlington County in the past, no case had ever been won. We were the first. After 18 months, the ordeal that began on an early Sunday morning was over. But the arrest of our two sons, the long, drawn-out helplessness and pain, the feeling that a lifetime of family values and beliefs were being questioned, the anger that my sons faced prison terms simply because of their skin color, cannot be forgotten. Neither can I forget that because we are black, it could all happen again.

Police Brutality Leads to a Loss of Trust in the Police

by Lawrence J. Finnegan Jr.

About the author: *Lawrence J. Finnegan Jr. is a judge for the New York Supreme Court and teaches ethics in criminal justice at St. John's University in Jamaica, New York.*

Two hundred years ago, Donatien Alphonse Francois was writing books and philosophical treatises, many of which focused on deviant sexual misconduct.

The infliction of enormous pain related to sexual activity was core to his sick beliefs. He is known as the Marquis de Sade, and the legacy of his thinking has left its mark on a few very sick individuals here in New York. Because of that sick thinking, a tough job has just gotten a lot tougher.

The police officers from New York City's 70th Precinct who allegedly committed a sadistic act of brutality against Abner Louima [who was sodomized with a toilet plunger handle in August 1997] have unwittingly allied themselves with criminals who belong in jail for life—criminals who will now find themselves the indirect beneficiaries of this reported police brutality.

Mistaken Beliefs

While New York is dismantling the 70th Precinct brick by brick, we should bury the refuse of that chamber of horrors along with the idea that there is no need for an independent monitor to watch the police. Lest we be misled by the swift action in moving against the accused officers, we should not delude ourselves in the belief these allegations are unique or isolated. Brutality is alive and well in this city; it has been for a long time.

With 38,000 police officers, 99-plus percent are as repulsed as anyone else by what has happened. The problem, past, present and regrettably for the future, is that many officers believe that this particular brutality went too far; not that brutality is in and of itself wrong. While it is true that only a handful of police would engage in such outrageous conduct, far too many are willing to tolerate lesser brutality in the warped belief that brutality earns respect. Even if just one

Lawrence J. Finnegan Jr., "Every Act of Brutality Looms Large," *Newsday*, September 11, 1997. Reprinted by permission of the author.

percent of the police force is capable of brutality, that leaves us with more than 300 officers who are willing to place their careers and reputations on the line, in order, in their view, to gain respect from the criminal.

What they fail to understand is that every act of brutality, rather than earning the respect of the criminal, is a license, even an invitation, for that criminal to inflict more pain on his next victim.

To pretend that the "blue wall of silence" is dead is as absurd as to think that brutality is isolated to one incident in the 70th Precinct. The best proof that the "blue wall" stands is the fact that the few officers who have come forward in the Louima case are under police protection themselves. Any chips in that blue wall are due only to the enormity of the exposure this case has brought and the intensity of government interest—albeit too late for past brutality—and don't represent a religious conversion, but a fear of going down with the wrongdoers.

A Loss of Trust

For those who don't see this act of sadism affecting them, just watch as we experience more and more not-guilty verdicts in this city. Cases that seem safe for prosecutors will increasingly result in acquittals as more and more jurors, white as well as all others, give the edge to the criminal in those marginal cases turning on police credibility. As a consequence, we all suffer from brutality in a way that affects the very quality of life that the police are supposed to be improving.

Only a truly independent board of investigation equipped with subpoena power, as recommended by the Mollen Commission in 1995 [the commission established by former New York City mayor David Dinkins in 1991 to study police brutality], will suffice to act as the eternal watch on those officers who opt for violence and vigilantism over respect for law, order and their oath of office. The police are not capable of policing themselves; no agency is, let alone one so shrouded in power and secrecy.

District attorneys are in no better position to initiate investigations. They work day in and day out with police and no district attorney looks to make his mark in society as the trumpeter of police malevolence.

"Cases . . . will increasingly result in acquittals as more and more jurors . . . give the edge to the criminal in those marginal cases turning on police credibility."

An independent, more anonymous body that has the personnel, the mandate and the power to investigate and deliver cases to a prosecutor has the best chance to succeed. The very opposition to such a concept by those who would be hurt most by it is the best test of its viability.

The thousands and thousands of good and decent police officers, who every day subject themselves to the wrath and rage of criminals and malcontents, suffer irreparable harm at the hands of a few bad officers.

It is now open season on the police for the next malcontent who comes along. We also can expect an inordinate amount of disingenuous brutality claims on the very police who do their jobs conscientiously.

Sadism truly defines what happened to Abner Louima. For the Marquis de Sade, criminally deviant acts were regarded as natural. He died in the prison lunatic hospital at Charenton 180 years ago. He left us the legacy of his name that has been given new meaning by some very sick officers in the 70th Precinct. While investigators continue to search the 70th Precinct they might look to find some of the Marquis' books.

In a few short years Abner Louima will be a wealthy man with a horrific memory. For most of our citizens, Abner Louima will be a distant memory, faded by time and the need to move on with our lives. Let's hope the enormity of the police and prosecution efforts to punish the wrongdoers will be sustained in all future acts of police brutality. We must hope that this new enlightenment is not a Pyrrhic victory for the truth for the moment.

Police Brutality Results in a Loss of Respect for the Police

by *Washington Afro-American*

About the author: *The* Washington Afro-American *is a twice-weekly newspaper in the Baltimore–Washington, D.C., area.*

Headlines in the local papers calling Terrence Johnson "a convicted cop killer" have done little to heal the wounds of our community. Unless the white media and others are willing to face the true facts in this case—and many other cases—we predict there will be more police killings, to the horror of all good thinking people.

Why is there so much hatred for police? Let's look at the facts.

(And we don't even have to mention the Rodney King beating case.)

Terrence Johnson

Terrence Johnson. He was only 15 years old and weighed about 98 pounds when he and his brother were stopped for a minor traffic violation in 1978. He was taken to a Prince George's County, Virginia, Police station, where in the presence of police of all races Terrence said:

"I was kicked in the groin. They all converged on me at one time. They kept kicking me and stomping me. There were six to seven police. I was thrown in a room and this officer had my neck in a headlock. I bit him in the chest. I was in so much pain. He kneed me in the stomach. I had my hand on his gun. I stepped back and shot him. I kept thinking that they were going to kill me. All I remember was shooting one time."

Two policemen died in this struggle. For this, Terrence Johnson was sentenced to 25 years in prison. He served 16 years before being paroled and then pardoned.

In early 1997, police say, he robbed a bank and as police approached they say

Reprinted from the March 8, 1997, editorial of the *Washington Afro-American*, "Facing Reality: Police Brutality Could Lead to Police Killings," by permission.

he killed himself. The white press reported the police were "jubilant."

Brian Gilmore wrote in the *Washington Afro-American* in March 1997:

"I live in D.C., but I am very familiar with P.G. County and its police. My experiences and all of my friends' experiences with Prince George's County cops is one of complete negativity. Two weeks after Terrence Johnson killed those cops, my friends and I were pulled over by P.G. cops and treated like dirt.

"They pointed shotguns at our heads, called us 'niggers' over and

> *"Each time an incident [of police brutality] happens somewhere there is a person who will look at a policeman not as a protector of society, but as an enemy of his people."*

over, dared us to try to escape so they could shoot us, kicked us in the legs, yelled in our faces, and then, after we had been reduced to nothing, they let us go. . . . Every Black man I know in this area has had one or more of these kind of experiences over the years with the P.G. police both before the double cop shooting and after."

The Wrong House

The *Holland vs. O'Brien* case now in the D.C. Courts:

The family charges that a police unit of 20 Black, white and Hispanic officers kicked in their front door. They say the officers were acting on an erroneous tip from an informant who had given the police three wrong addresses in the same neighborhood for a drug bust.

The family said the police kicked in the front door and acted like cops "out of control." "They threw furniture across the room, wrecked the whole house, and threw all of the food out of the refrigerator onto the floor. They threw the man of the house against the wall when he tried to tell them they had the wrong people."

The children in the family, who are honor roll students, are now under psychiatric care. All the police said was, "We went in the wrong house."

Each time an incident like this happens somewhere there is a person who will look at a policeman not as a protector of society, but as an enemy of his people.

No community can live safely with this kind of distrust and brutality.

Healing

We must heal. Those in the community who had put so much faith in the rehabilitation of Terrence Johnson must heal. Those who carry a hatred in their hearts because of what policemen have done in the past must heal. And policemen who are grieving over the killing of fellow officers must heal.

Somehow police officers must once again be seen in the eyes of all citizens as protectors of the people. The road ahead will not be easy, but a first step would be for all police officers to take a pledge to respect citizens' rights as they go about their difficult job. Yes, we need law and order, but policemen must not beat citizens in their custody; harass Black men just because they are Black; and abuse their authority. Each news story about police brutality undermines the work of thousands of good police and the citizens who want to be able to respect them. Respect breeds respect; brutality breeds brutality. It is as simple as that.

Police Brutality Makes Citizens Feel Less Safe

by Dianne Liuzzi Hagan

About the author: *Dianne Liuzzi Hagan is a freelance writer.*

The tragedy of Jonny Gammage's death in Brentwood, Pennsylvania, has touched all of America. [Gammage, who is black, was driving a Jaguar owned by his cousin, Pittsburgh Steeler Ray Seals, through a white neighborhood at night in October 1995. He was pulled over for a minor traffic violation by white police officers. Seven minutes later, he was dead by suffocation.] How could this have happened in America in 1995? More than that, how many African American men must die as they go about their normal course of business in their lives. It is frightening for those of us who have husbands, sons, fathers or brothers of color to think that one day we may receive the same phone call Jonny Gammage's family did on that tragic night.

Some of us were aware a long time ago that monsters such as Fuhrman, Koon and Vojtas exist. [Mark Fuhrman, Stacey Koon, and John Vojtas are all police officers who have been accused or convicted of police brutality.] Jonny Gammage's death in 1995 in Brentwood, Pennsylvania, was not a surprise, but one more episode in a long history of renegade cops who choose to abuse their power. They choose to bring their prejudices and hatred to their jobs, just as they choose who they will protect and who will pay the price.

I have witnessed bad cops in action. And I ask myself, do I feel safe? Do I feel protected under the law? Is my family protected? My children? And most of all, my husband? My husband is African American. He is hard working and a family man, but in the minds of many cops he fits the description of a criminal.

Not a Safe Feeling

During our freshman year of college on our first date, our car was pulled over by a police officer who wanted to know if I was in the car of my own free will. I was not struggling, screaming or otherwise acting out of sorts. But I am white; my husband is black. My future husband and I were simply out to enjoy some

Reprinted from Dianne Liuzzi Hagan, "Is It Safe?" *Interrace*, vol. 7, no. 1, 1996, by permission of *Interrace*.

time together; however, the police officer felt it was his duty to stop us and ask the question. We laughed it off after the cop left, but there was an uncomfortable difference in how we perceived the incident. He said he was used to it; I was stunned. Did I feel safe that evening?

A few years later, my husband was sitting on his parents' porch on a steamy summer night. A cop pulled over to the curb and demanded identification. When my husband offered to go into the house to get some, he was detained. After hearing a com-

> *"My husband is my safety net. . . . One renegade cop could change all that. It is something I fear . . . more than an accident on my husband's job as a fire fighter."*

motion, my future father-in-law came out in his pajamas and convinced the officer that my husband indeed lived in that house and was not, in the most passive way imaginable, robbing the poor inhabitants blind. Did my in-laws feel safe that evening?

Another time my husband was getting into our car, when he felt a gun at the back of his head. A police officer, stopping a potential car theft, reasoned aloud that blacks don't buy foreign cars. Did my husband feel safe that evening?

My husband was out walking late one night in our neighborhood, when a police car pulled up next to him and demanded to know what he was doing. When he said he lived in the neighborhood, the cop told him he was lying. The cop had grown up in the very same neighborhood, and he was sure no blacks lived there.

Finally, the cops told my husband that they had followed him and watched him peek in various windows along his walk on a street that my husband had not even crossed. Then they forced him in the back of the patrol car, repeatedly trying to hit his head on the edge of the door frame. They took him downtown and locked him in a holding cell without charging him and without allowing him to make one phone call. At last, I heard from him at 6:00 a.m. the next morning after I had frantically called every local hospital asking if a black male had been admitted to the emergency room. Do I feel safe knowing my husband cannot even walk in his own neighborhood?

More recently, my husband went to our daughters' school to pick them up. Several white adults passed by the cop on duty, who nodded pleasantly at each one. When my husband passed by, the cop stopped him and asked what his business was in the school. Do my children feel safe?

A Typical Experience

Our experiences are not atypical. Many other black males throughout the country have also experienced such harassment from police officers. Jonny Gammage's death is tragic. He was a good man, from our hometown of Syracuse, New York. A man who, even though he had gone on to become very successful, still gave back to his hometown and the children who live here. His uncle is a retired police officer. I look at the picture of Jonny's battered face and tears spring down my cheeks. Pain clutches my heart. I know what his family must feel. They have lost a son, a nephew, a sibling, a cousin and a friend. Do they feel safe? I know I don't feel safe. It could have been my husband who lay suffocating, broken and battered on a cold street because his skin is brown.

My husband is my safety net. He is my rock. One renegade cop could change all that. It is something I fear more than cancer, more than a car accident, more than an accident on my husband's job as a fire fighter. Should I feel safe?

The cops who killed Jonny Gammage should be tried for intentional homicide. They should be convicted and given life imprisonment without parole. They should be an example to other renegade cops that Americans of all colors won't tolerate their behavior. Only then can we *all* feel safe.

Chapter 4

How Can Police Brutality Be Reduced?

Preventing Police Brutality: An Overview

by Richard Lacayo

About the author: *Richard Lacayo is a senior writer for* Time *magazine.*

Police brutality works only in the dark. The sadistic assault on Abner Louima, the Haitian immigrant who was allegedly sodomized with a toilet-plunger handle by New York City police [in August 1997], was supposed to be confined to a station-house bathroom. But now that the attack is a public outrage—his injuries took him to the hospital, and from there to newspaper front pages—much more is at stake than just the reputation of Brooklyn's 70th Precinct, where four officers face charges. All around the country, the aggressive, "zero tolerance" policing strategy—which has contributed to New York's plummeting crime rate and is being imitated in other cities—is now getting a second look.

All but career criminals are happy with the nationwide drop in such crimes as murder, rape and assault. But the Louima attack, which is also an assault, has citizens wondering whether one kind of public order has been achieved at the cost of another. In short, is America's crackdown on crime bringing with it an increase in police brutality? The best answer, in most cities, is probably not—though harassment and violence against minorities remains endemic in some quarters. "This is a major problem in this country, particularly in urban areas," says Norman Siegel, executive director of the New York Civil Liberties Union [N.Y.C.L.U.]. In truth, no one keeps reliable national statistics. And local claims are suspect. A decline in complaints to local police review boards doesn't necessarily prove that there are fewer occurrences; critics say that such complaints in New York are down because abused citizens have given up. Despite more than 16,000 complaints against New York cops since 1993, only 180 officers have been disciplined, most of them with just a lecture or the loss of a vacation day.

But New York is not America. In fact, several police departments that entered the 1990s with a reputation as out-of-control head bangers, including Los Angeles and New Orleans, have turned a corner. That's because cities have learned to simultaneously provide effective police training, install a credible oversight authority, develop better relations with the people they serve and send a clear message to cops that abuses won't be tolerated.

It's a lesson learned the hard way. Six years after the Rodney King beating, Los Angeles is policed very differently. The L.A.P.D. has shown impressive progress. Its percentage of white officers has decreased from 61.3% in March '91 to 50% in July '97, producing a rank and file less likely to see a minority community as a hostile planet. The proportion of female officers, whom studies show are less prone to abusive behavior, has increased from 13.3% to 17.4% in the same time period. Citizen complaints are monitored by a new office of inspector general. "It's quite a different face on the Los Angeles police department," says Edith Pérez, president of the city's new police commission, a civilian body that oversees the 9,400-member department. Last Friday [August 22, 1997] the city swore in a new police chief, Bernard Parks, an African-American veteran of the force who promised to "provide a better service to the citizens."

> *"Cities have learned to simultaneously provide effective police training, install a credible oversight authority, . . . and send a clear message to cops that abuses won't be tolerated."*

What constitutes effective oversight of that service remains a big question. As a means for exposing and punishing police misconduct, civilian review boards have a mixed reputation. Many have no subpoena power and meager investigative staff, which leaves them powerless to get to the bottom of cases. While the New York board is supposed to be made up entirely of civilians, a majority of its members are former law-enforcement officials, prosecutors and lawyers. "What is needed is an independent board of civilians who are trained in investigating complaints," says N.Y.C.L.U. head Siegel.

In May [1997], a voter referendum approved just that kind of arrangement for Pittsburgh, Pa., but not before a prolonged local struggle, federal intervention and one highly publicized death nearby. Critics of the department say that by the late 1980s, police were out of control. "They were taking people off the street with absolutely no due process and throwing them in jail," says A.C.L.U. [American Civil Liberties Union] attorney Timothy O'Brien. At the same time, virtually every complaint that came before the department's internal-affairs division was dismissed.

Matters came to a head two years ago [1995] with the killing of Jonny Gammage, a cousin of Ray Seals, then star defensive end of the Pittsburgh Steelers. Gammage, 31, was driving Seals' Jaguar through a mostly white suburban neighborhood when he was stopped by police, ostensibly for driving erratically. After an officer knocked a cellular phone from Gammage's hand—he later claimed he thought it was a gun—officers pinned Gammage face down on the pavement. He later died of suffocation. Only three of the five suburban officers present went to trial. One was acquitted of involuntary homicide by an all-white jury. The case against the other two resulted in a mistrial.

Earlier this year [1997] the U.S. Department of Justice entered into a consent decree with the city of Pittsburgh in which the police department agreed to a litany of new procedures, including strict documentation of the use of force, extensive new training and the appointment of an outside auditor with access to police disciplinary records. The new Citizen Police Review Board will have the power to conduct its own investigations and subpoena witnesses.

Several police departments, including New York's, have also begun trying to identify problem officers early. That has been an important reform in New Orleans, where the police department has come a long way from October 1994, when Officer Len Davis ordered a lethal hit on citizen Kim Groves for filing a brutality complaint against him. On the same day Groves was killed, Richard Pennington was sworn in across town as the new superintendent of police. With the city's reputation in free fall, Pennington moved quickly to replace the department's discredited internal-affairs division with a more independent public-integrity division and to ban controversial restraining tactics such as choke holds and hog-tying.

Pennington also established an early-warning system that flags the records of cops who have drawn more than one complaint. Those officers get 40 hours of training in everything from their choice of words when making an arrest to the correct way to secure handcuffs. Says Pennington: "We jump on the problem and address it immediately."

"Less than 5% of all cops constitute the 'bad' element," says Ron Hampton, a retired Washington police officer who now heads the National Black Police Association. "But if the other 95% stand around and do and say nothing, that is where the real problem lies." The code of silence is formidable. For two days after Louima was assaulted in New York, no one in the 70th Precinct said anything about the incident. And even a department willing to act against bad cops is thwarted by police unions and civil service rules that allow officers to go over the heads of supervisors trying to discipline them. Boston police commissioner Paul Evans has complained that many of the officers he attempts to penalize for misconduct successfully appeal their punishments before the state's civil service commission.

> *"As a means for exposing and punishing police misconduct, civilian review boards have a mixed reputation."*

Two weeks ago [August 1997], however, a judge in Massachusetts' highest court provided police throughout the state with a compelling incentive to behave. He ruled that municipalities don't have to indemnify officers who break the law in pursuit of their duties. Says Boston police department spokeswoman Margot Hill: "[The city] can step back and say, 'You're on your own, kid.'"

The Louima case comes at the very moment when police departments around the country are fascinated by a crime-fighting strategy that New York's Mayor Rudolph Giuliani credits for much of his city's remarkable drop in crime. The zero-tolerance policy encourages police to focus on quality-of-life violations—public drinking, lewd behavior, loud music—as a means to discourage more serious crimes. The idea is that when left untreated, small disorders breed larger ones. The policy also goes by the name "broken windows," after the idea that one broken window on a street will encourage people to break more of them. Along with New York, such cities as Cleveland, Ohio, Milwaukee, Wis., and St. Louis, Mo., have adopted the approach.

Critics of the strategy say it encourages cops to sweep neighborhoods and harass ordinary citizens for minor offenses and opens the way to an us-vs.-them mentality. George Kelling, a Rutgers University professor who helped develop the idea, says it has gone awry in some places; it was intended to be carried out in the context of a larger strategy of community policing, the widely popular approach in which cops get out of squad cars to involve themselves in community problems. "Zero tolerance and 'sweeps' are not part of my vocabulary," says Kelling. There's plainly some tension between the confrontations required by quality-of-life enforcement and the kind of cooperation between cops and locals that community policing is intended to promote. How to resolve that is still a work in progress. "There is clearly a right and a wrong way to do broken windows," says Indianapolis, Ind., Mayor Stephen Goldsmith, whose city started adopting the strategy five years ago [1992].

In the end, none of the institutional machinery to discourage brutality works without a clear message from the top that bad cops are bad news. New York's Giuliani may have sent out the wrong signal even before he was elected. While still a candidate, he addressed a wild demonstration of 10,000 out-of-uniform officers who assembled outside city hall to protest the decision by then Mayor David Dinkins to establish the city's civilian review board. After taking office, Giuliani was repeatedly accused of dragging his feet on hiring investigators for the board. Last year [1996], when he tried to cut a fourth of the investigative staff, the city council said no.

An effective board is still a lot cheaper than an out-of-control police force. Louima, the victim in the latest assault, announced plans . . . to file a $55 million lawsuit against the city. Though in the past Giuliani has defended officers accused of egregious violence, in this episode he opted swiftly for the victim. He also announced plans for six months of town meetings between New Yorkers and every one of the city's 38,000 officers. Maybe all that talk could have been avoided if the cops had earlier heard a clearer statement about brutality from the mayor's office.

Radical Changes Are Needed to Counter Police Brutality

by People Against Racist Terror

About the author: *People Against Racist Terror publishes* Turning the Tide, *a quarterly journal of antiracist, antisexist, and antihomophobic activism, research, and education.*

The horrifying police torture of Abner Louima in New York City in 1997 has once again drawn media attention to the issue of police abuse, brutality, and corruption. But the media has focused exclusively on the forcible sodomy of this Haitian immigrant—by cops with a stick apparently from a toilet plunger which police then shoved in his mouth, breaking his teeth after they had torn his rectum, bowel and bladder. By excluding numerous other cases, including killings, not only in New York but around the country, this reinforces the police claim that such a horrifying incident is only an "unfortunate aberration." Nothing could be further from the truth.

Not an Isolated Incident

Consider the following incidents, not one of which was mentioned in a single news report or feature article on the torture of Louima. Within a week of that attack, a white cop in a suburb of Dallas, Texas, was acquitted of killing a 52-year-old mentally ill Black man. Police in the Los Angeles suburb of Bell Gardens shot and killed Alfieri Shinaia, 23, after he didn't raise his hands when they ordered him to, while they were serving a search warrant. Chicago police shot and killed Andrew Durham, 21, an unarmed Black man. Baltimore police shot and killed James Quarles, 22, an unemployed Black man holding a knife on the street while onlookers pleaded with them not to shoot. An off-duty cop in Philadelphia set his girlfriend on fire. And Nashville police shot and killed Leon Fisher, 23, leading to a night of rebellion in the Black community. Not

Reprinted from People Against Racist Terror, "The ABC's of Police Criminality: Abuse, Brutality, and Corruption, "*Turning the Tide*, Fall 1997, by permission of People Against Racist Terror, PO Box 1055, Culver City, CA 90232.

one of these incidents made the news outside of their local communities.

What these incidents make clear is that police abuse, brutality, and corruption are not isolated, not aberrations, but a serious, systematic, and ongoing problem that demands immediate, concerted, and uncompromising action on a national level. People Against Racist Terror (PART) has been involved for many years in the struggle to hold the police accountable for crimes they commit. Our perspective is that because of the colonial nature of United States society, the police function as an occupying army in oppressed communities, and as border guards in more privileged communities. In this context, we can understand why police abuse, brutality, and corruption is a growing problem.

> *"No single action, demonstration, or campaign is sufficient in itself to deal with this enormous problem."*

As the political and economic elite intensify their exploitation of workers and colonized people in the global economy and within the United States itself, the need for repression, imprisonment, and even the kind of torture visited upon Abner Louima is also increasing. The struggle against police brutality must take these realities into account. Such police repression is independent of the intentions or character of any individual officer. It is beyond any legitimate function of duly constituted and democratically controlled social protective forces. It speaks directly to the essentially undemocratic character of the political, social, and economic structure within which we live.

We understand that in this regard, the only true "good" cop is one who steps forward to blow the whistle on the perpetrators of police brutality.

Otherwise, the dichotomy between good cop and bad cop is simply a matter of tactical role-playing, which the cops habitually use in order to break the resistance of people whom they are interrogating. In other words, the good cop only serves to make the bad cop seem more intimidating, and the bad cop serves to make the "good" cop seem (falsely) like a friend or confidante. This basic strategy of the carrot and the stick is followed not only by the police but by all institutions of social, economic, and political control. Thus we see the two-party system, in which the parties take turns playing good cop and bad cop to various constituencies. It is the same strategy the CIA teaches in its torture manuals: that the alternation of pain and relief is more excruciating than the constant application of pain.

A Four-Point Program of Action

PART is proposing several points for action on a national level to deal with police abuse. We believe that this program can unite diverse forces from many different communities in the kind of concerted effort, based upon the principle of solidarity—that an attack against one is an attack against all—which is necessary to uproot not only police brutality but all forms of repression and colonial violence.

No single action, demonstration, or campaign is sufficient in itself to deal with this enormous problem. This means that a multitude of actions and approaches must be supported, coordinated, and combined so that our efforts reinforce each other to accomplish our goal. We must overcome sectarianism, organizational jealousy, and localism. All our best efforts are required.

Justice and Solidarity for the Victims

First, we must support and seek justice for the immediate victims of police abuse, brutality, and corruption. Also, we must build a community of resistance that embraces the families and friends of all such victims. Abner Louima deserves our loving support; and the police and political leaders responsible for his torture deserve our energetic outrage. This same love and outrage must also be made manifest in the cases of James Quarles, Alfieri Shinaia, Andrew Durham, Leon Fisher, and all of the many hundreds—indeed thousands—of people killed, maimed, and abused by the police every year. This requires an ongoing commitment, particularly by lawyers and other legal personnel, to challenge police abuses in the courts. It also demands community fund-raising efforts and other cultural activities, so that victims and their families will not be neglected or forgotten.

Watching the Watchmen

Second, we must develop a street-level capacity to monitor the police, in order to prevent the daily harassment, brutality, and intimidation of the community, particularly in communities of color, that make possible the more notorious killings and other atrocities. This would include such efforts as COP-Watch, which have begun in several cities, some under the auspices of Anti-Racist Action, others independent. Such direct action projects must be set up in many more cities and in many more communities.

They are the direct answer to the question "Who watches the watchmen?" which is as old as the Roman Empire and as contemporary as the American one. Until we can dispossess the exploiters and colonizers of their power, we must begin to exercise our own power. These efforts must be coordinated on a national level when they expose evidence of brutality or abuse. In addition, we need community education about people's rights vis-à-vis the police, so that the young people who are often the target of police hostility know their rights. Such efforts as the Alliance Working for Asian Rights and Empowerment (AWARE) in Orange County, California, which addresses police harassment and mug-shots of Asian-American youth, should be duplicated in other areas. Rights are only won and maintained through struggle.

> *"We must develop a street-level capacity to monitor the police, in order to prevent the daily harassment, brutality, and intimidation of the community."*

Community Control of the Police

Third, we need to incorporate into this struggle—to the extent possible without compromising principles—people who are not often directly victimized by the police, or who may think of the police as their protectors. In other words, white people, who have in the past supported the police in the majority, must be educated and struggled with about the true nature of policing in our society. This is a fundamental aspect of breaking reactionary solidarity on the basis of whiteness, of ending an identification with and as the oppressor. We have to educate people about the relentless, systematic nature of police abuse, brutality, and corruption. PART has been contributing to this educational effort by maintaining, along with several other police-accountability activists, an e-mail list that circulates incidents of police misconduct around the country. Almost every night, drawn from local mainstream media sources, we e-mail out from 5–15 articles about such police criminality and repressiveness around the country. A more systematic search, combined with better grass-roots monitoring and reporting, would amass such incontrovertible evidence that even those who blind themselves to police abuse would be forced to see, and to act. Understanding that there are material reasons in class, racial and national privileges for that willful blindness, nonetheless such exposures would begin to deny the police the political cover they currently enjoy, and force people to face the true nature of the system within which we live. It will challenge people to question not only the en-

> *"We have to educate people about the relentless, systematic nature of police abuse, brutality, and corruption."*

forcers, but the colonial laws which are being enforced, and our own collective position within that system of colonial law and imperial order.

One possible way to focus this awareness and action is through a political campaign for community control of the police, a demand first raised by the Black Panther Party. This demand for community control is an anti-colonial, anti-authoritarian demand. It is distinct from so-called community-oriented policing, which is a strategy being implemented in cities across the country under police auspices. That strategy, in the words of Jeff Church, a police proponent, in *Law and Order: The Magazine for Police Management,* does the same thing as what "the military calls changing an enemy or a population's thoughts[,] 'Psychological Operations,' or 'Psy-Ops.'" In other words, community-oriented policing is not a solution to the militarization of the police or its use as a domestic occupying army—it is a manifestation of a more sophisticated but still military strategy for waging that domestic counter-insurgency war. It is an example of liberals striving to be better guardians of the empire than conservatives.

Community control of the police, on the other hand, is a radical reform that would attempt to open a political and cultural space for anti-colonial struggle within the current system. It would involve elected boards of community residents who would have the power not simply to review "civilian" complaints, but to investigate, subpoena, and discipline or even dismiss abusive police. The campaign to create and institutionalize such community control boards would hopefully involve broader sectors of the population, as well as providing an opportunity to unite the various communities of Blacks, Asians, Latinos, and Native people who have been the principal victims of police brutality into a united front. It could drive a wedge between the corporate elite and neighborhood residents and businesses; between the power structure and at least some sectors of the white community that can be drawn into solidarity and unity with oppressed and colonized people.

National Unity in Action

Finally, we must make every sincere effort to unite existing, ongoing projects and campaigns. Right now, there is a National Coalition on Police Accountability, NCOPA, which mainly incorporates groups focused on civilian review boards, as well as some law enforcement professionals, especially Black and Latino cops, who are genuinely concerned about police abuse and have actually blown some whistles and testified about racist harassment both within police departments and against community residents. At the same time, there is a national effort initiated by the Center for Constitutional Rights, and incorporating many committees for justice for individual victims of police murder and brutality. . . . The October 22nd Coalition to Stop Police Brutality, Repression and the Criminalization of a Generation, initiated by the Revolutionary Communist Party, but which has drawn participation from many concerned individuals and organizations including Food Not Bombs, the National Lawyers Guild and the Coalition Against Police Abuse (CAPA) in L.A., [held] a . . . national day of protest in cities across the country. October 22 marks the anniversary of the police frame-up arrest of anarchists Sacco and Vanzetti which culminated in their execution almost 75 years ago.

We must strive to overcome the differences in political culture and ideology that have separated these efforts. We cannot allow such differences to impede our efforts, when the need for action is so urgent; it would be criminal. None of the named campaigns or coalitions puts forward the consciously anti-colonial politics that guide PART in our efforts against racism and police brutality. Nonetheless, PART has endorsed and supported all of these campaigns and coalitions. Only such a non-sectarian approach will give us a chance of success against the forces of reaction and state repression.

The Police Must Be Subject to Community Oversight

by American Civil Liberties Union

About the author: *The American Civil Liberties Union is a national organization that works to defend civil rights guaranteed by the U.S. Constitution. The following viewpoint is excerpted from their publication* Fighting Police Abuse: A Community Action Manual.

The bad news is . . . police abuse is a serious problem. It has a long history, and it seems to defy all attempts at eradication.

The problem is national; no police department in the country is known to be completely free of misconduct. Yet it must be fought locally; the nation's 19,000 law enforcement agencies are essentially independent. While some federal statutes specify criminal penalties for willful violations of civil rights and conspiracies to violate civil rights, the United States Department of Justice has been insufficiently aggressive in prosecuting cases of police abuse. There are shortcomings, too, in federal law itself, which does not permit "pattern and practice" lawsuits. The battle against police abuse must, therefore, be fought primarily on the local level.

The Good News

The good news is . . . the situation is not hopeless. Policing has seen much progress. Some reforms do work, and some types of abuse have been reduced. Today, among both police officials and rank and file officers, it is widely recognized that police brutality hinders good law enforcement.

To fight police abuse effectively, you must have realistic expectations. You must not expect too much of any one remedy because no single remedy will cure the problem. A "mix" of reforms is required. And even after citizen action has won reforms, your community must keep the pressure on through monitor-

Excerpted from the American Civil Liberties Union, *Fighting Police Abuse: A Community Action Manual* (New York: ACLU, 1997). Copyright 1997, American Civil Liberties Union. Reprinted with permission.

ing and oversight to ensure that the reforms are actually implemented.

Nonetheless, even one person, or a small group of persistent people, can make a big difference. Sometimes outmoded and abusive police practices prevail largely because no one has ever questioned them. In such cases, the simple act of spotlighting a problem can have a powerful effect that leads to reform. Just by raising questions,

> *"Police brutality hinders good law enforcement."*

one person or a few people—who need not be experts—can open up some corner of the all-too-secretive and insular world of policing to public scrutiny. Depending on what is revealed, their inquiries can snowball into a full-blown examination by the media, the public and politicians. . . .

A Civilian Review Board

Civilian review of police activity was first proposed in the 1950s because of *widespread dissatisfaction with the internal disciplinary procedures of police departments.* Many citizens didn't believe that police officials took their complaints seriously. They suspected officials of investigating allegations of abuse superficially at best, and of covering up misconduct. The theory underlying the concept of civilian review is that civilian investigations of citizen complaints are more independent because they are conducted by people who are not sworn officers.

At first, civilian review was a dream few thought would ever be fulfilled. But slow, steady progress has been made, indicating that it's an idea whose time has come. By the end of 1997, more than 75 percent of the nation's largest cities (more than 80 cities across the country) had civilian review systems.

Civilian review advocates in every city have had to overcome substantial resistance from local police departments. One veteran of the struggle for civilian review has chronicled the stages of police opposition as follows:

• *The "over-our-dead-bodies" stage,* during which the police proclaim that they will never accept any type of civilian oversight under any circumstances;

• *The "magical conversion" stage,* when it becomes politically inevitable that civilian review will be adopted. At this point, former police opponents suddenly become civilian review experts and propose the weakest possible models;

• *The "post-partum resistance" stage,* when the newly established civilian review board must fight police opposition to its budget, authority, access to information, etc.

Strong community advocacy is necessary to overcome resistance, even after civilian review is established.

What Is Civilian Review?

Civilian review systems create a lot of confusion because they vary tremendously. Some are more "civilian" than others. Some are not boards but municipal agencies headed by an executive director (who has been appointed by, and is accountable to, the mayor).

The three basic types of civilian review systems are:

• *Type I. Persons who are not sworn officers conduct the initial fact-finding.* They submit an investigative report to a non-officer or board of non-officers, who then make a recommendation for action to the police chief. This process is the most independent and most "civilian."

• *Type II. Sworn officers conduct the initial fact-finding.* They submit an investigative report to a non-officer or board of non-officers for a recommendation.

• *Type III. Sworn officers conduct the initial fact-finding and make a recommendation to the police chief.* If the aggrieved citizen is not satisfied with the chief's action on the complaint, he or she may appeal to a board that includes non-officers. Obviously, this process is the least independent.

Although the above are the most common, other types of civilian review systems also exist.

Why Is Civilian Review Important?

• *Civilian review establishes the principle of police accountability.* Strong evidence exists to show that a complaint review system encourages citizens to act on their grievances. Even a weak civilian review process is far better than none at all.

• *A civilian review agency can be an important source of information about police misconduct.* A civilian agency is more likely to compile and publish data on patterns of misconduct, especially on officers with chronic problems, than is a police internal affairs agency.

> *"Many well-intentioned police officials have failed to act decisively against police brutality because internal investigations didn't provide them with the facts."*

• *Civilian review can alert police administrators to the steps they must take to curb abuse in their departments.* Many well-intentioned police officials have failed to act decisively against police brutality because internal investigations didn't provide them with the facts.

Principles for an Effective Civilian Review Board

1. *Independence.* The power to conduct hearings, subpoena witnesses and report findings and recommendations to the public.
2. *Investigatory Power.* The authority to independently investigate incidents and issue findings on complaints.
3. *Mandatory Police Cooperation.* Complete access to police witnesses and documents through legal mandate or subpoena power.
4. *Adequate Funding.* Should not be a lower budget priority than police internal affairs systems.

5. *Hearings.* Essential for solving credibility questions and enhancing public confidence in process.
6. *Reflect Community Diversity.* Board and staff should be broadly representative of the community it serves.
7. *Policy Recommendations.* Civilian oversight can spot problem policies and provide a forum for developing reforms.
8. *Statistical Analysis.* Public statistical reports can detail trends in allegations, and early warning systems can identify officers who are subjects of unusually numerous complaints.
9. *Separate Offices.* Should be housed away from police headquarters to maintain independence and credibility with public.
10. *Disciplinary Role.* Board findings should be considered in determining appropriate disciplinary action.

The existence of a civilian review agency, a reform in itself, can help ensure that other needed reforms are implemented. A police department can formulate model policies aimed at deterring and punishing misconduct, but those policies will be meaningless unless a system is in place to guarantee that the policies are aggressively enforced.

Civilian Review Works

Civilian review *works*, if only because it's at least a vast improvement over the police policing themselves. Nearly all existing civilian review systems
• reduce public reluctance to file complaints
• reduce procedural barriers to filing complaints
• enhance the likelihood that statistical reporting on complaints will be more complete
• enhance the likelihood of an independent review of abuse allegations
• foster confidence in complainants that they will get their "day in court" through the hearing process
• increase scrutiny of police policies that lead to citizen complaints
• increase opportunities for other reform efforts.

A campaign to establish a civilian review agency, or to strengthen an already existing agency, is an excellent vehicle for community organizing. In Indianapolis, for example, a civilian review campaign brought about not only the establishment of a civilian review agency, but an effective coalition between the Indiana American Civil Liberties Union (ACLU), the local branch of the National Association

> *"Civilian review can alert police administrators to the steps they must take to curb abuse in their departments."*

for the Advancement of Colored People (NAACP) and other community groups that could take future action on other issues.

Your community's campaign should seek a strong, fully independent and accessible civilian review system. But even with a weak system, you can press for changes to make it more independent and effective.

Considerable progress has been made in the area of police misconduct in the use of deadly force. Although the rate of deadly force abuse is still intolerably high, national data reveal reductions in the number of persons shot and killed by the police since the mid-1970s—as much as 35–40 percent in our 50 largest cities. This has been accompanied by a significant reduction in the racial disparities among persons shot and killed: since the 1970s, from about six people of color to one white person, down to three people of color to one white.

> *"Police leadership typically looked the other way when officers were involved in questionable incidents."*

This progress serves as a model for controlling other forms of police behavior. And was achieved through hard work and perseverance. In the mid-1970s, police departments began developing restrictive internal policies on the use of deadly force. They adopted the "defense of life" standard: the use of deadly force only when the life of an officer or some other person is in danger. In 1985, the Supreme Court finally upheld this standard in the case of *Tennessee v. Garner.* However, the majority of policies adopted by police departments go beyond the Court's *Garner* decision, prohibiting warning shots, shots to wound and other reckless actions. Most important, these policies require officers to file written reports after each firearm discharge, and require that those reports be reviewed by higher-ranking officers.

How to Control Police Shootings

To [control police shootings], your community must:

• Ensure that the police department has a highly restrictive deadly force policy. Most big city departments do. But the national trend data on shootings suggest that medium-sized and small departments have not caught up with the big cities, so much remains to be done there. Much remains to be done as well in county sheriff and state police agencies, which have not been subject to the same scrutiny as big city police departments.

• Ensure enforcement of the deadly force policy through community monitoring. To be accountable, the police department and/or the local civilian review agency should publish summary data on shooting incidents.

Citizens should also be able to find out whether the department disciplines officers who violate its policy, and whether certain officers are repeatedly involved in questionable incidents. . . .

Reduce Police Brutality

Your community's principal aim here should be to get the police department to adopt *and enforce* a written policy governing the use of physical force. This policy should have two parts:

• It should explicitly restrict physical force to the narrowest possible range of specific situations. For example, a policy on the use of batons should forbid police officers from striking citizens in "non-target" areas, such as the head and spine, where permanent injuries can result. Mace should be used defensively, not offensively. The use of electronic stun guns should be strictly controlled and reviewed, since they have great potential for abuse because they don't leave scars or bruises.

• The policy should require that a police officer file a written report after *any* use of physical force, and that report should be automatically reviewed by high ranking officers.

Your community's second objective should be to get the police department to establish an early warning system to identify officers who are involved in an inordinate number of inappropriate physical force incidents. The incidents should then be investigated and, if verified, the officers involved should be charged, disciplined, transferred, retrained or offered counseling, depending on the severity of their misconduct. The Christopher Commission's report on the Rodney King beating in 1991 ascertained that L.A. police leadership typically looked the other way when officers were involved in questionable incidents, a tolerance of brutality that helped create an atmosphere conducive to police abuses. . . .

Oversight of Police Policy

Police policies should be subject to public review and debate instead of being viewed as the sole province of police insiders. Open policy-making not only allows police officials to benefit from community input, but it also provides an opportunity for police officials to explain to the public why certain tactics or procedures may be necessary. This kind of communication can help anticipate problems and avert crises before they occur.

The Police Review Commission (a civilian review body) of Berkeley, California, holds regular, bi-monthly meetings that are open to the public where representatives of community organizations can voice criticisms, make proposals and introduce resolutions to review or reform specific police policies.

> *"Open policy-making . . . provides an opportunity for police officials to explain to the public why certain tactics or procedures may be necessary."*

The Police Practices Project of the ACLU of Northern California successfully pressured the San Francisco Police Department to adopt enlightened policies regarding the treatment of the homeless; the use of pain-holds and batons; the deployment of plainclothes officers at protests and demonstrations; intelligence gathering; the selection of field training officers, and AIDS/HIV education for police officers. The Project has also prevented the adoption of an anti-loitering rule, a policy that would have made demonstrators financially liable for police costs, and other bad policies.

In Tucson, Arizona, a Citizens' Police Advisory Committee was incorporated into the city's municipal code in July 1990. Composed of both civilian and police representatives, it has the authority to initiate investigations of controversial incidents or questionable policies, and other oversight functions. . . .

Keep your eye on the big picture. On the one hand, each individual reform is only one step on a long road to correcting the deeply entrenched problem of police misconduct; on the other hand, important and genuine reforms can be won.

A well-organized, focused campaign against police abuse can draw broad community support. The key is to transform that support into realistic demands and develop strategies that turn those demands into concrete reforms.

Civilian Review Boards Must Police the Police

by Lynne Wilson

About the author: *Lynne Wilson, an attorney in Seattle, writes frequently about police accountability issues.*

"I had been in internal affairs investigations a couple of times, and they were very easy to breeze through. I answered a few questions. I lied through every answer, and I went back to patrol."

—Former New York City police officer Michael Dowd

On August 21, 1994, Moises DeJesus was arrested by police officers patrolling Philadelphia's largely Latino 25th District. Handcuffed in the back of a patrol car, the 30-year-old suspect had a "mental fit or seizure," said Gerard McCabe, an attorney for Philadelphia's newly formed Police Advisory Commission (PAC), "and started kicking out the windows to get air." He was then allegedly beaten in the head by the officers, lapsed into a coma, and died three days later. After the district attorney refused to press charges against the officers, Latino community leaders demanded an inquiry. DeJesus' death in police custody became the first major case for the recently formed Philadelphia PAC and sparked the citizen oversight commission's first public hearing. The investigation also set off an all out war on the Philadelphia PAC by the local Fraternal Order of Police (FOP) Lodge No. 5.

The FOP attacked on three fronts. First, when PAC investigators began questioning officers about the DeJesus incident, FOP President Rich Costello simply declared that members of his organization would not cooperate or respond to subpoenas or interview requests. Second, the FOP filed suit in Pennsylvania state court to shut down the advisory commission for lack of legal authority. Third, the FOP succeeded in having two bills presented in the state legislature: one (the "Law Enforcement Officers' Bill of Rights") would undermine PACs by prohibiting citizen questioning of officers; another would dismantle all of the state's PACs entirely.

Lynne Wilson, "Cops vs. Citizen Review." *Covert Action Quarterly*, Winter 1995/1996, by permission of the author and *Covert Action Quarterly,* 1500 Massachusetts Ave. NW, #732, Washington, DC 20005; phone: (202) 331-9763; e-mail: caq@igc.apc.org. Annual subscriptions payable by check, money order, or credit card (VISA/MasterCard): U.S. $22; Canada $27; Europe $33.

The Struggle for Citizen Review

Strong antagonism by police toward citizen oversight boards is not new. Even though the boards have only advisory and limited investigatory authority, and can never undertake disciplinary action, most police and the organizations representing them resent "outside interference." Law enforcement agencies, they insist, can and should police their own through existing internal affairs procedures. In almost every state, police agencies are legally required to have a mechanism for the receipt and investigation of citizen complaints, particularly those involving improper use of force.

These mechanisms have often served more to protect the police code of silence than the public interest. In the 1960s, public outrage over widespread police misconduct against the Black Panthers and anti-war demonstrators in the San Francisco Bay area sparked a movement to institute "citizen review" oversight. The powers of these commissions, which sprang up around the country, ranged from the authority to launch independent citizen investigations with full subpoena power, to a mandate limited to the review of investigations completed by sworn officers.

By late 1994, 66 external complaint review bodies had been established, a 400 percent increase over the 13 that existed in 1980. Sixty percent of major urban areas were included. This growth parallels the emergence of organized police accountability groups such as the National Coalition on Police Accountability (which had its first meeting in 1984) and the International Association for Civilian Oversight of Law Enforcement. Another factor has been the increasing clout of the National Black Police Association, which endorses citizen review. In addition, as police theorists and managers promote "community policing" to get a handle on crime, citizen review has gained support among key politicians. Many mayors and city council members see it as integral to returning officers to "the beat."

> *"Strong antagonism by police toward citizen oversight boards is not new."*

Finally, as major urban areas fall under clouds of police corruption and racism, citizens are demanding, and getting, more oversight. In 1995 in New York City, for example, the Civilian Complaint Review Board (created in 1993 by the City Council) reported an alarming increase in brutality complaints, with 450 cases a month. Police brutality suits have cost the city $87 million since 1992 and payments are rising sharply. The board is investigating a major police corruption scandal directly related to drug trafficking in which scores of officers in the Bronx and Harlem have recently been convicted and discharged. The District of Columbia also created a Civilian Complaint Review Board which had independent investigative resources, the power to subpoena records, and authority to hold public hearings. It was disbanded in 1995, ostensibly because of lack of funds. A new proposal is in the works.

Similarly, 13 years ago, New Orleans city officials created an Office of Municipal Investigations (OMI), a citizen-run agency with explicit subpoena and investigative powers. According to OMI Director Peter Munster, serious criminal charges against New Orleans police officers have increased in the last few years with more than 50 officers arrested, indicted, or convicted on charges including rape, aggravated battery, drug trafficking, and murder. One officer, who continues to work at a desk job, is the prime suspect in a series of prostitute murders, said Munster. Another officer was recently convicted of gunning down her former partner during an armed robbery, committed off-duty. She now faces the death penalty. Although some of these charges stemmed from investigations by the OMI, its role in exposing the extent of corruption and stemming its spread was limited.

When Is a Union Not Quite a Union?

Even when the boards are relatively ineffective, concerned citizens see the existence of a review mechanism as an essential step in curbing the widespread racism, brutality, and impunity which characterize many law enforcement agencies. Most police unions, on the other hand, oppose them on principle—as a threat to their civil and labor rights.

The issue of labor rights and use of the term "union" to describe police groups is problematic. Technically, an organization of police officers formed to negotiate with management for the wages, benefits, and working conditions of its members is a "labor union." Police unions, however, are unique in three fundamental ways: First, the right of police officers—alone among workers—to use physical, and sometimes even deadly, force requires public accountability to ensure that this power is not abused. Furthermore, because they are responsible for public safety and cannot lawfully strike, police unions have won unique concessions from management, including heightened due process protections. And finally, unlike members of any other labor union, police act as the tools of management against other unions. Recently, for example, scores of officers in full riot gear escorted scab workers to the strike-bound Detroit Newspaper Agency (DNA) print shop and used clubs, batons, and pepper spray on picketing strikers. The DNA paid $500,000 to the Detroit suburb of Sterling Heights for police overtime and expenses.

"As major urban areas fall under clouds of police corruption and racism, citizens are demanding, and getting, more oversight."

Nonetheless, because of their status as private labor groups, police unions operate under a veil of secrecy, totally outside the realm of democratic controls such as public decision-making or public disclosure laws. It is this secrecy, combined with their members' paramilitary discipline and skills, that makes police organizations so powerful, so dangerous, and so difficult for those working toward police accountability to oppose.

But even though elected or appointed police chiefs and sheriffs *always* have the final word on whether or not a particular officer is disciplined—regardless of who does the investigating—civilian boards can exert strong pressures. Especially with respect to use of excessive force allegations, community oversight agencies not only receive far more allegations than do internal mechanisms, but they sustain them more often.

Police Union Resistance: A Tactical Overview

It is not surprising, then, that the FOPs and police unions—paramilitary labor organizations whose purpose is to protect the interests of their patrol officer members—will go to great lengths to eliminate oversight. The tactics that police organizations increasingly use illustrate some of the ways in which they differ from other trade unions. They also show how difficult it is to distinguish genuine labor grievances from attempts by police to avoid accountability. As in Philadelphia, police organizations around the country are developing an increasingly sophisticated array of tools designed to manipulate the political system and sabotage the citizen review boards. At least five categories of tactics are being implemented.

National Level Organizing

"I wasn't political when I came out of the FBI," says Charles Kluge, a former agent who is current executive director of Philadelphia's PAC, "[but] some of the political stuff has been very eye-opening." Over the past decade, police unions have become extremely politicized and have established a national lobbying presence. In October 1994, for example, the National Association of Police Organizations (NAPO) founded the "National Law Enforcement Officer Rights Center" in Washington, D.C., "to protect officers' legal and constitutional rights that are being infringed upon by a wave of anti-police civil litigation."

> *"A review mechanism [is] an essential step in curbing the widespread racism, brutality, and impunity which characterize many law enforcement agencies."*

NAPO's main objective appears to be passage of a national "Law Enforcement Officers' Bill of Rights Act" which attempts to weaken state and local review by allowing only commissioned police officers to conduct investigations. NAPO claims that the bill, sponsored by Sen. Joseph Biden (D-Del.), is collectively supported by its 475,000 police officer members, by the Fraternal Order of Police, and by the International Brotherhood of Police Officers.

Litigation Sabotage

On the state and local level, police response to perceived incursions on their autonomy follows a pattern. John Crew of the American Civil Liberties Union's

(ACLU) Police Practices Project, has identified three stages of union resistance to citizen oversight:

• "Over My Dead Body." After a particular, usually racially charged, incident prompts serious community discussion of citizen oversight, police leaders threaten to resign or take other extreme action.

> *"The right of police officers . . . to use physical, and sometimes even deadly force, requires public accountability to ensure that this power is not abused."*

• "Political Inevitability." When a visible pattern of abuses emerges, police leaders suddenly undergo a "magic conversion," and become proponents of citizen oversight—advocating a pallid model lacking such teeth as subpoena power and independent investigations.

• "Post-Partum Litigation." If a community manages to obtain strong citizen oversight, even if only on paper, police union resistance becomes vehement. Increasingly, unions are initiating lawsuits (such as that currently under way in Philadelphia) challenging the underlying authority or legality of the citizen review process. In California such lawsuits are common, even though many California boards have been operating for up to 20 years, and even though, says the ACLU's Crew, these suits have been "100 percent unsuccessful. In not one single legal challenge have the unions won."

If chilling citizen oversight is the goal of these unwinnable . . . suits, chilling citizens' complaints is the predictable result of another union tactic. In the fall of 1994, the Seattle Police Officers Guild slapped defamation suits against six citizens who had filed complaints that were not upheld by the department's internal investigations section. The suits were apparently prompted by the citizen review auditor's recommendation that officers who had logged a certain number of unsustained complaints be required to undergo intensive supervision. Although the guild's suits were ultimately dropped, citizen complaints in Seattle dropped almost 75 percent in the next six months.

Obstructionist Tactics

When faced with a citizen review board which has independent investigative powers, leaders of police unions often advise their members to refuse or avoid subpoenas or interviews, to plead the Fifth Amendment, or to otherwise block an inquiry. This obstructionism is illegal, according to Crew. Although officers cannot be forced to testify if they plead the Fifth Amendment, they can be disciplined or discharged for their refusal. Police unions, says Crew, invoke these tactics even though they know that they will not win in court and that review boards have the legal power to compel statements. The effect of the obstructionism—and of . . . suits against citizens who file complaints—is time-consuming and expensive litigation; the goal is to create enough pressure to force cities and counties to back down.

State Legislation and Lobbying

Law enforcement groups use their significant political clout, based largely on financial resources. According to a 1992 study by California Common Cause, law enforcement groups in that state contributed $1.2 million to local lawmakers between 1989 and 1991. "[L]aw enforcement groups also hold the potent weapon of campaign endorsements," the study noted. ". . . If legislators vote against bills supported by police interests, they know they run the risk of being labeled as 'soft on crime,' even if the legislation has nothing to do with public safety. The last thing a legislator wants in an election year is to lose the endorsement of police groups, or worse yet, wind up on their hit list."

In California, and other states, law enforcement groups have used this clout to pass a "Police Officer Bill of Rights" that grants privileges to cops during disciplinary processes—privileges not available to suspects whom the same officers may have arrested or questioned. The "Bill of Rights" proposed in Pennsylvania, for example, restricts non-department questioning of officers and prohibits anonymous complaints. Others require that complaints be removed from personnel files after a few years and restrict the types of behavior that can trigger disciplinary action.

In 1992 and again in 1995, California legislators proposed major amendments to that state's Bill of Rights Act imposing a one-year statute of limitation from the time of the complaint to the date of punitive action. Given normal backlog and lengthy appeal delays, this limit would have virtually guaranteed immunity from discipline. Massive organized opposition from the ACLU and other groups defeated the proposed legislation.

Administrative Challenges over Collective Bargaining

Although sometimes they lose sight of it, the primary purpose of police organizations is to represent members as public employees and to collectively bargain with municipal and state governments over such negotiable issues as wages, benefits, off-duty pay, hours, and promotional opportunities. Since 1986, when the federal Fair Labor Standards Act was applied to public employees, most police unions have argued that the issue of citizen involvement in individual officer discipline falls under collective bargaining and thus involves only two parties: the union and the employer. This position, according to Clyde W. Summers, omits entirely the role of a public justifiably concerned that police "will act abusively or unlawfully and that their superiors will not take appropriate disciplinary action." The Ohio Supreme Court has recognized this right of the public to participate. Since collective bargaining is not an "appropriate process for the full consideration of the issues raised in a complaint by a citizen against a police of-

> *"Police chiefs and sheriffs* **always** *have the final word on whether or not a particular officer is disciplined."*

129

ficer," it ruled, effective citizen review is essential to maintaining the public trust and disciplining police abuses.

Not all rulings have been as sympathetic to public involvement. In 1992, the Spokane (Washington) City Council established a citizen review process giving citizens the right to appeal whenever the police chief refused to discipline an officer after a complaint. The police union fought back with a complaint to the state's Public Employment Relations Commission. It alleged that the City had unilaterally changed procedures and by publicly disclosing disciplinary information, had invaded the officers' privacy rights, something that "inherently constitutes a working condition."

> *"Police organizations around the country are developing an increasingly sophisticated array of tools designed to . . . sabotage the citizen review boards."*

The Employment Relations Commission agreed with the union that changes in disciplinary procedures were subject to collective bargaining. It ordered the city to dismantle the Citizens Review Panel and to negotiate with the union. Spokane did not appeal this ruling and set out to work with the police body to create a new oversight mechanism—one that includes police representatives, holds secret hearings, and has no subpoena power.

On the other side of the country, the same scenario is being played out. The Syracuse (New York) Police Benevolent Association has filed a similar complaint against the Citizen Review Board. A decision by the New York Public Employees Relations Board (PERB) is pending. "The most dangerous aspect of all this," says community activist Nancy Rhodes who edits *Policing by Consent*, "is that we have no access to the process. The PERB hearings are conducted in secret as are the union negotiations. There are no democratic controls."

Philadelphia: An All-Out Citizen Review War

In Philadelphia, too, the FOP is clearly in full-blown "post-partum" resistance—sparked by the DeJesus case, but fueled by the potential effectiveness of the city's citizen review mechanism. Created in October 1993 after a fierce political struggle, it has subpoena power, independent investigators, and the power to conduct public hearings. After it was funded and staffed in late 1994 and took on the DeJesus death-in-custody as its first case, the local FOP began to actively sabotage the PAC investigation.

Few cities are more in need of citizen oversight than Philadelphia. At about the same time the FOP was challenging citizen review, six of its members pled guilty to federal charges stemming from blatant corruption in Philadelphia's largely African-American 39th District. *The New York Times* described the convicted cops as "so corrupt, so calloused to the rights and welfare of residents that the details have shaken the city to its roots." Federal charges include conspiracy, obstruction of justice, and "pocketing more than $100,000 in cash they robbed from suspected drug dealers through beatings, intimidations, illegal searches and denying suspects their constitutional rights." Revelations from this latest in a series of police scandals will force the city to set aside at least 1,400 drug-related convictions and pay millions of dollars for false arrest and imprisonment claims.

An FBI investigation of Philadelphia's Police Department, started in 1992 in the 39th District, now includes the department's Highway Patrol, as well as other areas, including the predominantly Latino 25th District, where DeJesus died. Even Ken Rocks, vice president of the local FOP, admitted that the prospect of the arrest of additional officers was certain and "very, very distressing."

Still, the FOP maintains that the police can police themselves. The case of officer John Baird makes nonsense of that claim. Baird, who had made thousands of arrests in the 39th District by the time of his discharge, had received excellent ratings from his superior officers, while he was racking up 22 citizen complaints—all dismissed. By the 23rd complaint, Baird "was confident that the whole thing would go away, just as the previous 22 complaints had." His downfall was bad timing. The last complaint was filed in March 1991, just as the Rodney King case prompted the Justice Department to review all police brutality cases, including those in Philadelphia. The resulting FBI investigation and arbitration hearing revealed Baird's sordid history of fabricating evidence, buying off witnesses, and lying and covering up.

It also came out that over the past five years, Philadelphia's Police Internal Affairs Unit had investigated almost 600 citizen complaints. Only ten were sustained, with only two Philadelphia officers actually disciplined. The "enormous bias" in the department and its almost total inability to deal with a department run amuck was undeniable, according to *Philadelphia Inquirer* reporter Mark Fazlollah.

Nonetheless, the FOP refuses to cooperate with an agency whose main purpose is to bolster public trust in the police. And community leaders in Philadelphia, particularly those in the Latino community, continue to demand that the Police Advisory Commission function in the public eye to deal with rogue officers. "The Commission is the only hope that our community has to redress the wrongs of some of the officers from that District," says one 25th District Latino leader. Another community leader hopes that the DeJesus hearings "will begin a cleansing process that in the long run will restore the community's confidence in a critical public service. Hopefully, something positive will come out of the DeJesus tragedy."

> *"Police officers should not be entitled to a separate 'Bill of Rights' that encourages disregard of the real thing and promotes an official sense of separateness and privilege."*

Some of the demands by police unions, including the right to due process during any disciplinary proceeding, deserve active citizen support. Others far exceed the boundaries of legitimate labor concerns: Police officers should not be entitled to a separate "Bill of Rights" that encourages disregard of the real thing and promotes an official sense of separateness and privilege. In addition, contrary to the administrative ruling in Washington state, the daily working conditions of police are not affected by citizen review since boards only *recommend* discipline to a police chief who then decides whether or not to act. At least one state supreme court has upheld this position.

As the situation in Philadelphia illustrates, unions have the resources to launch innumerable chilling lawsuits. They can obstruct and sabotage, refuse to cooperate, and take the Fifth. But in the end, when the situation festers to the point that it has in Philadelphia, citizen oversight and democracy have a chance to reassert themselves.

The Police Must Be Involved in Their Communities

by National Association for the Advancement of Colored People

About the author: *The National Association for the Advancement of Colored People is the oldest and largest civil rights organization in the United States.*

There must be serious change in the very concept of policing in our cities and towns. The first change must be to do away with the "us versus them" dynamic of police-community relations. This drawing of lines—and more, this taking of sides—only fosters racism and violence, and it needs to be altered.

There was much testimony throughout the six National Association for the Advancement of Colored People (NAACP) hearings held in 1991 in Norfolk, Los Angeles, Miami, Houston, St. Louis, and Indianapolis on the police being outside or above the community. There was much testimony about an insular police culture that disparages all outsiders, particularly those in minority communities. There was considerable testimony by members of the African American community about the racial animosity that is part and parcel of the "us versus them" mentality.

The sides as drawn hold the police out as the good guys and everyone else—especially those of color—as the bad guys. This is the sort of outlook that fosters police disregard of the constitutional rights of young black people. This is the sort of value system that spawns police perjury. This is the ideology that fosters an apartheid-like experience for all African Americans in the inner city. Paradoxically, the "us versus them" view held by so many officers fosters the kind of anger and hostility toward the police that leads to violence directed against them and to police killings.

We recognize that changing the conception of the police as an occupying force in the community will not happen easily or quickly. There is no single program that can be instituted or policy that can be adopted that in and of itself

Excerpted from *Beyond the Rodney King Story: An Investigation of Police Misconduct in Minority Communities*, by the NAACP (Baltimore: NAACP, 1995). The publisher wishes to thank The National Association for the Advancement of Colored People for authorizing the use of this work.

can transform the nature of police-community relations. The commitment to change must be made at all levels in the police department and in local and national government. It must be demonstrated concretely throughout police department policies, practices, and programs. Efforts to improve police-community relations must receive both financial and moral support from elected government. Similarly, it will take an ongoing, active effort to participate in finding solutions to collective problems, whether as part of the police force or as residents of the community.

Serving Their Community

Police officers must integrate themselves into the community. The presence of outsiders with weapons, policing a community they neither know nor understand, perpetuates the notion of police officers as an occupying army. Roots in the community, or at least a commitment to developing roots, must be seen as an important hiring criterion.

A witness in Houston described the reasons for police to be part of the community:

> [M]any of the policemen do not live in [the] City of Houston. And that is part of the problem. Even when I was growing up, I did know all the policemen. . . . And they lived in the neighborhood, and we knew them. And we also—we knew that we could get in trouble with them, and they would also come to our parents and say whatever they thought about the kids' behavior. But the policeman [*sic*] today have no connection and no relationship with the neighborhood.

Though the idea is in some aspects controversial, we join a number of those who testified at the hearings in strongly recommending that officers be required to live within a short commuting distance from where they work. A number of police departments have some sort of residency requirement. If police officers reside in or near the neighborhoods in which they work, they will come to know the other residents as people. Once they come to know their neighbors, they will find both similarity and difference. They will be forced to acknowledge the humanity of those whom they police. In addition, there might be a corollary benefit to blighted inner-city neighborhoods in maintaining a pool of middle-class residents.

"The presence of outsiders with weapons, policing a community they neither know nor understand, perpetuates the notion of police officers as an occupying army."

We also recommend that police officers be required, as part of their job, to participate in community-related endeavors. There are an infinite number of choices: public school activities; recreational sports programs; the Girl and Boy Scouts; the Big Brother/Big Sister program; teenage pregnancy centers; drug rehabilitation programs; centers for the elderly; women's centers; rape crisis offices; gay and lesbian rights centers; AIDS hotlines and programs; classes in

English as a second language; immigrant centers; programs for the physically disabled; offices for the mentally ill; and centers for the mentally retarded.

Police Officers as Social Service Providers

Police officers must be reconceptualized as public servants engaged in social service delivery. Notwithstanding their current paramilitary image and structure, this was the original conceptualization of the police. Officers have always been urban "helpers," providing information, directing other municipal services to areas of need, and serving as an essential neighborhood resource.

The stereotype of the police function as catching criminals and fighting crime has always reflected only a small part of the police role. The stereotype is firmly planted in the minds of both law-enforcement officers and the general public, and it has been cultivated by the police themselves.

> *"If police officers reside in or near the neighborhoods in which they work, they will come to know the other residents as people."*

This is the "Lethal Weapon" image of police in America; it pervades our popular culture in books, on television, and at the movies. This image has an enormous influence on the organization, staffing, and operation of police agencies.

While crime fighting will always be an important part of police work, it is not the only police function, nor is it necessarily the most important one. In inner-city areas, police perform the widest array of services. Here, Herman Goldstein writes, the combination of poverty, unemployment, dilapidated housing, poor education, and homelessness results in police officers being called on to serve as

> surrogate parent or other relative, and to fill in for social workers, housing inspectors, attorneys, physicians, and psychiatrists. It is here, too, that the police most frequently care for those who cannot care for themselves: the destitute, the inebriated, the addicted, the mentally ill, the senile, the alien, the physically disabled, and the very young.

Why not reconceptualize the police as part of the "Urban Corps," an inner-city version of the Peace Corps? Other members of the corps could include firefighters, social workers, community mental health professionals, health care providers, public school teachers, drug and alcohol addiction counselors, and youth counselors. The "Urban Corps" could focus on long-term, multidisciplinary solutions to crime, polarization, and urban decay. One rarely, if ever, hears of widespread tension between the community and firefighters. No doubt the reason is that firefighters are seen as providing an essential service, without taking anything from the community. Citizens are not afraid of them.

Police officers must, at the same time, be reconceptualized as important, valuable members of the community, essential to a free society. Police should be seen as the keepers of the calm, the keepers of safety. What could be a more important social role? Police ought to be compensated for their work to an extent commensurate with its value. Revaluing police work ought to be part of a massive rethinking of a number of undervalued occupations, such as public school teaching, public health care provision, and legal representation of indigent people.

Greater Police Accountability

Effective management of any large bureaucracy requires systematic, formalized, and comprehensive mechanisms to ensure attainment of the organization's goals and objectives. Among the most important are mechanisms to achieve *accountability*—rewarding and encouraging positive police behavior, as well as preventing, mitigating, and improving negative police performance.

This may be more important for the police bureaucracy than for any other because, as the Christopher Commission wrote in its 1991 *Report of the Independent Commission on the Los Angeles Police Department*, the police "are given special powers, unique in our society, to use force, even deadly force, in the furtherance of their duties." As enforcers of the law, they are not only an agent of the values our society deems most important, they are the most visible barrier between civilized society and its alternatives.

It is axiomatic, as the Christopher Commission pointed out, that "the right to use force carries with it a heavy responsibility not to abuse it." When armed law enforcers engage in use of excessive force, abuse of power, or "merely" rude or discourteous behavior, the injury is not only to individual citizens but to the Constitution, our sense of community, and our collective sense of dignity.

> *"Police officers must be reconceptualized as public servants engaged in social service delivery."*

In a time of enormous social change—in racial and ethnic composition, economic direction, family structure, suburban-urban relationships, and the role of government—we must be especially vigilant to uphold, and not to take for granted, the social balance of power. Police must serve the community; community members must not become the servants, tools, or whipping boys (and girls) of the police.

It is essential that those at the top, police leaders and managers, devise control mechanisms that work. According to the Christopher Commission, it is also essential that

> leadership . . . be comprehensive and constant, not isolated or sporadic. They must make their weight felt throughout the system—from recruitment, through training, promotion, assignment, and discipline. . . . To make genuine progress on issues relating to excessive force, racism, and bias, leadership must avoid sending mixed signals. . . . Leniency in discipline or easy forgiveness . . . will be misread as condoning improper practices.

The leadership of the police department must make clear both the rules of conduct and the consequences for violation of the rules, whether the misconduct is by actual behavior, by ignoring the improper conduct of other officers, or by failing to supervise. . . .

Diversity in Hiring

There is no question that police officers should be more like the communities they serve, a recommendation made by many who testified at the NAACP hearings throughout the country. Almost all the police officials who testified at these hearings presented their department's affirmative action plan, emphasizing successes in recruiting, hiring, and promotions, and apologetically explaining the failures. There was an almost universal view that diversity in the police ranks was a key to bettering police-minority relations and to stopping police brutality.

There are a number of concerns, however. First, the picture of a wholly black police force in wholly black neighborhoods perpetuates racial segregation on every level. The Rodney King incident and the unrest that followed were not unrelated to Los Angeles's status as one of the most racially segregated cities in the United States.

Second, there is something a bit worrisome about black expansion in police hirings in the last twenty years as compared to other occupations. Between 1970 and 1990, African Americans took 41.4 percent of new police positions. In that same period, blacks took only 7.4 percent of new pharmacist positions, 10.1 percent of new health official positions, and 12.7 percent of new electrician positions. Policing is quite literally a blue-collar job. Policing also has a very public profile, and is increasingly associated with the black "underclass" that is so heavily policed.

While affirmative action plans and a serious commitment to diversity in the police must be part of any recommendation for change, affirmative action and diversity are not a panacea. Police culture runs deep. While the figures seem to show that police officers of color tend to commit fewer acts of police brutality, and less severe forms of it, it is not true that African American officers never assault or abuse African American citizens.

It has not seemed to matter historically that police officers tend to come from the working class: when confronted with a choice of identifying with that class or carrying out their duties as police officers in a way that was destructive to members of the working class, the police always identified as police. Why do we think that African American police officers, when confronted

> *"Police officers should be more like the communities they serve."*

with a conflict in identity—African American or police—would see themselves as African American first? Will they profit from that identification professionally? Personally? In a society that devalues and degrades African American identity, why would a police officer embrace that identity first?

Central to police culture is a dichotomy: "us versus them." There is nothing complex about the line drawing. It is not "some-of-us versus them" or even "most-of-us versus them." There may be a cost to African American police offi-cers who dare to be African Ameri-can first. A commitment to a diverse police force must be accompanied by a commitment to changing police culture.

> "*Community-oriented policing has the potential to change the relationship between the police and the community.*"

Most police departments have done better with bringing minorities and women into the force at the bottom levels than in promoting minorities and women to positions of leadership and power. Diversity in police leadership is essential to changing the face of policing. . . .

A Community-Oriented Policing Approach

Every police department represented at the NAACP hearings referred to its commitment to "community-oriented policing." Norfolk calls its program PACE (Police Assistance Community Enforcement), while the program estab-lished by the St. Louis Metropolitan Police Department is called COPS (Com-munity Oriented Policing Services). The Miami and Metro-Dade Police Depart-ments have a number of programs, all considered some form of "community policing."

Along with many who testified at the hearings, we strongly recommend a community-oriented approach to policing. We applaud those police depart-ments that have embraced such an approach, and we encourage them to con-tinue the work. The problem with efforts so far is that they appear to be piece-meal and extraordinary, rather than integrated into the scheme of the entire policing enterprise.

Community policing is a radically different approach to crime and other ur-ban problems from what we think of as "traditional" policing. Community policing seeks to address not only crime but *fear,* perhaps an even more crip-pling societal epidemic. It also seeks to address such diffuse social problems as community and racial tension.

Between the deep-seated causes of crime on the one hand and serious, violent crime on the other "lies a vast world of mundane friction and hurt," according to Malcolm K. Sparrow et al. in *Beyond 911.* This is where fear, tension, and community disorder take root and grow:

> Disorder and neglect—aggressive, drunken panhandlers, threatening youths, walls sullied by gang graffiti—often seem to signal that an area has been aban-doned to the forces of decline, and can be an even stronger trigger for fear than crime itself. Disputes—inside families, between landlords and tenants, employ-ers and employees, black and white neighborhood basketball teams, delivery

drivers and other road users—can cut at the fabric of social and community life and often develop into assaults and other crimes. Social and medical emergencies—runaways, the homeless, the dangerously ill clothed and ill fed—are serious on their own merits and frequently lead to victimization and crime.

Community policing means more than educating the public about the work of the police department, the dangers of drug abuse, or crime prevention. Community-oriented policing means actively engaging the community in defining problems, setting priorities and goals for the police, and finding solutions to community problems. Foot patrol is a central part of this approach. Getting police officers out of their patrol cars and onto the streets to meet the people who live there has proven to be good for crime prevention, good for community peace of mind, and good for police morale.

Community policing has also been called "problem-oriented policing." The theory behind problem-oriented policing is that a few common underlying conditions and problems lead to seemingly distinct police incidents. In order to understand the incidents, police officers must examine their causes in the broadest possible way. Police should go beyond criminal justice methods, like arrest, and explore other avenues.

Problem-oriented policing is proactive, not reactive. With the focus on patrol to prevent crime and "rapid response" to catch criminals, modern police have become increasingly isolated and reactive. Studies show that by the time officers arrive at a crime scene, no matter how quick the response time, it is generally already too late. Many crimes are discovered only when victims return to their cars or homes to find them stolen or broken into. Rapid response may provide some comfort to the victim, but it is often not enough to prevent the crime or to catch the perpetrator. In crimes where the victim is confronted by the perpetrator, rapid response has proven equally insufficient. If the victim/witness waits more than five minutes to call the police, the perpetrator will be gone. In Kansas City, only 2 percent of the police department's serious crime calls were thought to merit a rapid response. This finding is not unique to Kansas City.

Community policing and problem-oriented policing have much in common. Both seek to balance reactive and proactive strategies, responding to crises and emergencies but also responding to what the community wants and needs. Both encourage creativity and flexibility in dealing with complex urban problems. Both prefer specialization and focus over coverage of vast geographic areas. Both favor decentralization of police command. Both seek a police-community partnership.

Community-oriented policing has the potential to change the relationship between the police and the community, and to have some impact on the layered antagonism that spawned the Rodney King incident and the many other examples of violence and degradation testified to in the hearings. Community policing means to defuse the insider/outsider vision of the police, to overcome police resistance to change, to chip away at police culture.

Public Officials Must Denounce Police Brutality

by David N. Dinkins

About the author: *David N. Dinkins was the mayor of New York City from 1990 to 1994. In the following viewpoint, Dinkins refers to Rudolph Giuliani, who succeeded Dinkins as mayor of New York City in 1994 and was reelected in 1997.*

The horrific brutalization of Abner Louima [by police officers in the New York Police Department in August 1997], and the silence of officers and supervisors during and immediately after the incident, has created public outrage, and rightly so. Yet police violence, which has resulted in the severe injury or death of individuals who have not even been charged with a crime, takes place in our city with disturbing regularity—and the silence surrounding these incidents reaches to the highest level of city government. Tragically, the mayor [Rudolph Giuliani] has failed to pay attention—or to actively discourage violent tactics—until this most recent incident in an election year.

Police Brutality Was Ignored

In the past, the mayor has consciously ignored or dismissed the issue of police brutality, thereby contributing to a climate in which it could flourish unchecked. Even today, the usually exacting chief executive, rather than immediately demanding to know the exact circumstances surrounding this event, simply says that he would "like to know" why it took an hour and a half to secure a police escort to take the severely injured Mr. Louima to the hospital.

I was advised by Richard Roberts, Chief of the Criminal Section, Civil Rights Division, Department of Justice, that there is an open file on the Louima matter, that the FBI is investigating, and its civil rights office is in communication with the U.S. Attorney for the Eastern District in New York.

When I speak of the abuse of police power, as I have on many occasions since 1994, I always say that the vast majority of the women and men of the NYPD are good, honorable, hardworking people who put their lives on the line every

Reprinted from David N. Dinkins, "Giuliani Time: What the Mayor Must Do About Police Brutality," *The Village Voice*, August 26, 1997, by permission of the author.

day for the rest of us. They have a tough and dangerous job. And I am pleased with the record drop in crime in New York, which began in 1992 and continues today, thanks in part to their excellent work, and thanks in part to our Safe Streets, Safe City criminal justice program, which put more cops on our streets and offered young people alternatives to antisocial and illegal behavior.

Yet many New Yorkers feel less safe than they did a few years ago. Civilian complaints against police for excessive force rose by 61.9 per cent in 1995 compared to 1993. Abuse-of-authority allegations soared by 86.2 per cent, and allegations of illegal

> *"In the past, the mayor has consciously ignored or dismissed the issue of police brutality, thereby contributing to a climate in which it could flourish unchecked."*

searches skyrocketed by 135 per cent. That this particular kind of complaint has risen the most is very likely a reflection of increased brutality and illegal arrests. Nineteen ninety-six complaint figures are similarly high, and I submit that the only reason they haven't continued to escalate further is loss of confidence in the Civilian Complaint Review Board (CCRB), not a reduction in actual incidents, as recent reports would seem to indicate. Former CCRB executive director Hector Soto and many others believe that people simply don't file complaints any longer because they know, rightly so, that it is virtually useless to do so.

Aggressive Policing Is Not the Cause

The administration has told us time and again that complaints are the inevitable result of more arrests and a more assertive assault of quality-of-life offenses. But aggressive policing is *not* the cause, as anyone can discover by reading CCRB reports. They reveal that the majority of abuse allegations involve officers on routine patrol, in incidents that never result in arrests. The complaints come from people who are not only *not* arrested, but not even *ticketed*. In past years, only 30 per cent of civilian complaints involved no arrest or crime, or even suspicion of arrest or crime. Clearly, complainants are largely innocent bystanders who get caught up in illegal police behavior.

I will offer another disturbing statistic: more than half the complainants whose race is known are African American. About another 25 per cent are Latino. Altogether, 80 per cent of complaints are registered by people of color. Too often in our city, a young person of color, wearing his cap sideways, with the seat of his trousers down around his knees, is slammed against a wall and searched without cause, in serious violation of constitutional rights, as set forth in *Terry v. Ohio*. If nothing is found, he is told, "Have a nice day."

Some officers believe that because some of these "stop-and-frisks" do uncover weapons or drugs, there is sufficient justification for violating people's constitutional rights. But too often the wrongdoers end up going free because the evidence is suppressed, as it must be under our Constitution when there is an illegal search.

I charge that our police department, following the lead of this mayoral administration, is dangerously close to adopting a philosophy that the end justifies the means.

That there is alienation between our cops and the communities they serve is clear. I was pained to read the words of the Bronx officer quoted in *New York*, who said, "You couldn't pay me enough" to live in New York City, and told us, "The truth is I just don't want to have anything to do with" the people "down there." I was pained, but not surprised.

For such attitudes are not actively discouraged. Police misconduct is not consistently condemned. The violation of constitutional rights is not regularly denounced. Such messages say to officers whose inclination may be to misbehave: you can take such liberties, you can overstep the line, you are above the law.

Silence Speaks Volumes

For example, in the Kevin Cedeno case, the mayor hastily spoke and acted on the basis of unconfirmed police evidence that the 16-year-old victim had been shot in the stomach. When the medical examiner declared that the boy had been shot in the back, the mayor—rather than demanding to know why he and the public had been misinformed by police eyewitnesses—instead lectured the media. He said the press should have been asking what the boy was doing out at that late hour of the night, why he had a 22-inch machete, and what his criminal record was. All of this is of interest—but none of it is relevant to being shot in the back.

> *"Police misconduct is not consistently condemned. The violation of constitutional rights is not regularly denounced. Such messages say to officers ... you are above the law."*

Furthermore, as far as I know, no action was taken against the police eyewitnesses who provided the misinformation.

At a town hall meeting, a woman stood to ask a question of then–police commissioner William Bratton. She was the mother of the young man named Anthony Baez, who died as a result of an officer's illegal chokehold after that young man's football accidentally bounced into a police car. The police commissioner told the grieving mother she was making a fool of herself and should sit down. The mayor, standing right next to his commissioner, said nothing. His silence spoke volumes.

The officer involved in the case, Francis Livoti, had been the subject of about a dozen civilian complaints. Had he been appropriately disciplined, young Baez might well still be alive. In his nonjury trial over the Baez incident, the presiding judge referred to the "nest of perjury" built by the police witnesses, without whose truthful testimony the prosecution could not prove guilt. In a department trial, Livoti was found guilty of having used a chokehold and dismissed. But once again, as far as I know, the witnesses to the incident—including one supervisor, a sergeant—have faced no disciplinary actions. Officer Livoti is finally to be tried for an incident in which he slapped a young man who had his hands raised, then placed him in an illegal chokehold.

Our mayor may belittle the blue wall of silence today, but his previous silence may well have enforced its foundations.

The Civilian Complaint Review Board

It is troubling—yet not surprising—that in the face of persistent brutality, the administration slashed the CCRB's budget and appointed a board whose majority is not committed to taking action against brutality. Members who were committed to this mission were driven out.

Incidentally, properly funding and staffing the CCRB, thereby sending a message to cops who might be brutal, could *save* the city money. The city's civil-suit payments to the victims of police malfeasance have risen dramatically. The total for one fiscal year, 1994, was *$25 million,* and the comptroller tells us that a deluge of new cases is now being filed.

Ironically, one reason my administration's effort to create an independent board may originally have succeeded was thanks to the infamous Patrolmen's Benevolent Association City Hall "rally" in 1993. Then-candidate Giuliani, under the guise of seeking to calm the crowd, egged on the officers in what became a near riot, with police officers running atop vehicles, using foul and abusive language, and blocking the nearby Brooklyn Bridge. With regard to the kind of message the mayor sends officers, he has at least been consistent.

Many of us have long contended that brutality and corruption must be deterred by a comprehensive, rigorous system of monitoring and discipline. However, in a development particularly painful to those of us who fought long and hard for an independent Civilian Complaint Review Board, it is now swamped with cases and unable—or, in some cases, unwilling—to do its job. Some now suggest that we don't need the CCRB because it doesn't function. But what we need is a board that is *able* to function.

Today, complaints are so backlogged that in many instances, by the time the investigation is completed, the 18-month statute of limitations has been reached, and no action can then be taken against an abusive officer. In many cases in which investigators do finish their inquiry, substantiate allegations, and recommend action to the board in a timely fashion, the board fails to follow the recommendations.

> *"Equitable and appropriate discipline would help institute a fairer and more just police department."*

And when the board *does* vote to adopt the recommendations that allegations be substantiated, it must pass the findings to the police commissioner for actions—unless a crime has been committed, in which event the district attorney has jurisdiction. The police commissioner then has but two options, suspension for 30 days or dismissal. Nothing in between. In May 1997, I testified before the City Council to urge passage of a law that would provide additional options between these two extremes.

In many cases, no action *at all* is taken against officers. In the first six months of 1996, of 159 *substantiated* cases referred to the department for possible disciplinary action, charges were filed against only *one* officer. A second was subjected to "command discipline," which generally means loss of vacation time. One case was dismissed, 26 cases were dropped for lack of evidence, seven were dropped in 1996 and 43 the year before because the statute of limitations ran out.

> "The silence of good people in the face of brutality has enabled atrocities to continue."

Further, in at least one case when the CCRB substantiated a complaint of excessive force and recommended disciplinary actions, those employees involved in the investigation were dismissed.

A Deeply Troubling Picture

The statistics about brutality paint a deeply troubling picture. The individual suffering of the victims of brutality is even more distressing.

Consider the young man whom an officer kicked so hard in the groin that the victim had to have one testicle surgically removed. The officer was found guilty at a departmental trial. His penalty? Thirty days' suspension without pay. He was also put on probation for one year. When a Bronx district attorney later found out about the case, he had the officer indicted for felonious assault. A conviction means dismissal, which should have been the penalty imposed in the first place. Note that the mild department discipline was not the mistake of some low-level NYPD employee—final penalties are decided by the commissioner and his first deputy.

The Mollen Commission to Investigate Allegations of Police Corruption, which I appointed, recommended changes in the administrative code to provide further disciplinary options for the police commissioner, and several of the commission's proposals were embodied in the legislation before the City Council. However, I urge that we adopt the full extent of the commission's sensible measures to make discipline more effective, which were based on recommendations of former police commissioner Raymond Kelly, "to insure that legal technicalities do not allow corrupt officers to 'beat the system.'"

Proposals to End Police Brutality

Among the Mollen Commission proposals were:
• a minimum period of 90 days' notice before an officer is permitted to retire with full pension, to allow a sufficient time to complete disciplinary proceedings before an officer can escape the consequence of misconduct;

- the revocations of lifetime pension benefits for officers convicted of a felony in performance of their duties;
- the restorations of the statute of limitations for disciplinary proceedings to three years from the current 18 months;
- demotion in rank and salary for sergeants, lieutenants, and captains who have engaged in corruption or failed to carry out their supervisory duties (current law precludes such demotions);
- additional disciplinary options for the police commissioner, including suspension without pay for up to one year, monetary fines of up to $25,000, and demotion in grade or title with a commensurate reduction in salary;
- requiring arresting officers to attest to circumstances of arrest under penalties of law relating to false written statements.

These are hardly radical measures, and it seems to me that all good cops, and all New Yorkers, would support them. Serious and fair-minded attention to police brutality is not "anti-cop." Equitable and appropriate discipline would help institute a fairer and more just police department, increasing public confidence in the integrity of officers and the department.

> "Officers must obey the law, and their commissioner and mayor must give clear notice that lawlessness among cops will not be tolerated."

I must also add that the Mollen Commission found a correlation between corruption and brutality—not that every corrupt cop is brutal or every brutal cop is corrupt, but that there was a significant correlation. So the commission recommended an independent body with broad subpoena power to monitor and discipline police behavior. Such a board would go a long way toward eradicating and preventing a culture of brutality and corruption, establishing independent oversight and accountability. It would offer good cops the opportunity and the means to report the behavior of bad cops without fear of retributions. Today, that kind of forum does not exist.

Reform Is Not a Priority

The City Council passed legislation providing for an independent investigative and audit board with subpoena power. But the mayor vetoed that legislation. The City Council overrode the veto with 41 votes. The mayor refused to abide by the law, saying such a board would encroach on executive power. The matter went to litigation, and the mayor's position was upheld at an appellate level. The mayor insists that such a law would impinge on his prerogative, because the City Council would be allowed to recommend appointments.

Unfortunately, creating a climate for change in police culture and attitude does not seem to be a priority for this administration.

It's been said many times: the tone of the city is set from the top. And everyone knows that this mayor takes the leading role at One Police Plaza. As the election nears, the mayor may be changing his tune. But his past silence on discouraging and punishing police brutality has rung loud and clear.

Silence Encourages Evil

I frequently observe that the silence of good people in the face of brutality has enabled atrocities to continue—from the Holocaust to the internment of Japanese to brutal political repression today. Too many good people were silent when a ship named *The Saint Louis*, filled with people trying to escape Nazi Germany, was turned away by American immigration authorities in 1939. Too many good people were silent just a few years later, during World War II, when 142,000 Japanese Americans were imprisoned and their property confiscated, solely because of their ethnic heritage—a fate, it is important to note, that did not befall Italian Americans or German Americans.

> *"Fostering an environment in which [the police] feel they can ride roughshod over the rights of the innocent only erodes safety and people's trust in the law."*

Too many good people were silent when a form of legalized slavery was instituted in South Africa, and then many of them remained silent throughout the entire period of apartheid. Too many good people were silent, and remained silent, as the United States government shamefully rejected Haitian refugees. If they made it through the shark-infested waters, they were confined in something akin to concentration camps, while those from elsewhere in the world were greeted with open arms and resettlement assistance.

Indeed, would the pen held by the framers of the Constitution have left their mark of blood if the rest of the world had firmly and vocally opposed the tyranny of slavery?

I do not compare police violence to the horrors of the Holocaust or slavery, which resulted in the subjugation and death of millions. I am simply making the point that words—and action—are important. That it is when good men and women speak up and act that we succeed in bringing justice to bear. Like a number of others, I have written and spoken about this issue many times since 1994: in a *Daily News* op-ed in April 1995; in a televised speech before the City Club in April 1996; in hearings before the City Council in June 1997, to name a few instances.

Discipline the Police

It is my hope that the message may finally reach our mayor and the public loud and clear. Officers must obey the law, and their commissioner and mayor must give clear notice that lawlessness among cops will not be tolerated. Offenders must be fairly tried, and punished when appropriate. Independent oversight and command accountability must be established, as the Mollen Commission recommended, and police integrity must be fostered from the day cops enter the academy to the day they return their badges and guns. Such measures would institute lasting reform.

Finally, since a large percentage of complaints involve members of minority groups, a city residency requirement for officers is essential. Today in New York, over 40 per cent of our 38,000-member police force reside outside the city, and while all of them are not like the Bronx cop quoted in *New York*, we must ensure that fewer officers view the communities in which they work as alien, and fewer residents view the police as alien.

Encouraging cops to be more assertive against crime can be good. But fostering an environment in which they feel they can ride roughshod over the rights of the innocent only erodes safety and people's trust in the law.

The Police Must Be Held Accountable for Their Actions

by John DeSantis

About the author: *John DeSantis is a reporter for United Press International and the author of* The New Untouchables: How America Sanctions Police Violence.

The social climate has changed in the few years since people first cringed at the videotape of the beating Rodney King received on a Los Angeles street in 1991. Death and destruction visited southern California once again in 1994, when an earthquake ravaged highways and homes and claimed almost as many lives as the Rodney King riots. In the wake of that cataclysmic event, it appeared that issues of race and class and abuse of authority were made invisible by the shadows of helping hands extended from one Angeleno to another. As would be expected, the various local police departments performed admirably, providing whatever assistance they could to alleviate the tragedy's immediate effects. A police officer, in fact, was one of the first fatalities.

In other parts of the country, many police departments seemed to have become more aware of the dangers that could come from looking the other way from the problem of police violence. National police organizations continued their efforts to professionalize their member departments, encouraging ranking officials to take steps that might prevent abuse of force, and to take proper disciplinary action against offenders.

Whether this new post-King consciousness has resulted in an overall decline of brutality complaints or incidents nationwide is difficult to gauge. In some cases the King incident might have spurred officials to take even deeper cover when questionable cases arose, out of fear of public criticism or civil disorder. There is still no central, national clearinghouse for reports of such incidents or their dispositions.

The Outlook Remains Bleak

The outlook for true reform in the area of abuse of force remains bleak, because those with the greatest power to force change in policy, procedure, and law have chosen to remain silent. The failure of the federal legislation that attempted to address police violence is proof of this.

The Clinton administration, despite its seemingly benign public pronouncements, offers little hope for reform either. One of the most egregious uses of force by law enforcement officers in the past century occurred within the first few months after Bill Clinton took office, when a standoff between federal authorities and heavily armed Branch Davidian church members in Waco, Texas, ended with a literal firestorm that claimed the lives of several adults and children. The ill-

> *"The outlook for true reform . . . remains bleak, because those with the greatest power to force change in policy, procedure, and law have chosen to remain silent."*

fated and ill-conceived initial raid on the compound was itself a tragedy, resulting in the deaths of four highly dedicated and motivated Bureau of Alcohol, Tobacco, and Firearms (ATF) agents handpicked for the assignment from the New Orleans field office. The deaths of the Branch Davidians and their children only compounded the scope of the misadventure, and there has been little accountability demanded by the government or the public to whom it answers for the government's decision to storm the compound, precipitating the inferno.

Demanding Accountability

Attorney General Janet Reno said that she was taking responsibility for the catastrophe, but her mea culpa seems to amount to little more than a pronouncement of regret. There was little organized public criticism of Reno, nor was there much in the way of demand to know who was *truly* responsible for the Waco holocaust—at least not when compared with the furor surrounding another highly publicized case. New York's Hasidic Jewish community has demanded that the Justice Department investigate the death of Yankel Rosenbaum, the Australian rabbinical student who was killed in the early stages of the Crown Heights riots in New York City in 1991.

Brooklyn District Attorney Charles Hynes and other officials continually pressured Reno to launch a federal civil rights investigation into Rosenbaum's death, which she finally—grudgingly, it would seem—agreed to early in her stewardship at the Justice Department, in March 1993. Difficult as it is to bring actions in cases where government employees such as police officers are accused of civil rights violations, the prosecution of private citizens for such offenses is even more problematic. Experts at the attorney general's office may have felt—perhaps quite rightly—that such an investigation would result in little of value, and would serve only to be symbolic. Symbolism, however, can often serve an important purpose; if nothing else, a full-scale federal investigation into the Rosenbaum case could ease fears among members of New York's Jewish community that they are not equally protected by this country's laws. The case would never have received federal attention, however, without the intense pressure.

Using RICO to Prosecute Police Brutality

Legal experts have said it is possible that the inability of the attorney general to seek pattern or practice bans through the courts could be overcome, on a case-by-case basis at least, through inventive use of the Racketeer Influenced Corrupt Organizations Act, known as the RICO law. Putting together a civil RICO case against a police department that evinces a pattern of abuse through commission of specific crimes—such as murder or the intimidation of a witness—would be a difficult and controversial task, but could be seen as one of the weapons in the Justice Department's legal arsenal. That is, it could be if someone there wanted to stem police abuses badly enough. But little that is new should be expected from the Department of Justice in the way of police brutality prosecutions. If there will be no official accountability for the deaths of the children and adults in Waco, then how can the Department of Justice be expected to set the example for local and state law enforcement agencies and officials when an unarmed drug dealer is shot under questionable circumstances?

The public has become ever more preoccupied with the fear of crime, with renewed calls for the death penalty in states that currently prohibit its imposition. How could one expect outcries from the public against police brutality when its existence is denied or excused, or glanced at with a knowing wink that says, "We know you shouldn't have done it, but we're glad to be rid of him anyway?" One octogenarian in New York, upon seeing the Rodney King videotape, surprised her family and friends when she blurted out, "Why didn't they shoot the son of a bitch with the camera?" As Judge Jon O. Neuman has pointed out, the victims of police brutality are often the people whom the rest of society wishes would go

> *"How could one expect outcries from the public against police brutality when its existence is denied or excused, or glanced at with a knowing wink?"*

away. The current social climate would seem to tend toward a secret dark desire for summary dispatch of felons with extreme prejudice.

A Tragic Indifference

And yet, in most of the cases, the dead and injured were not gun-toting felons with innumerable scuff marks from justice's revolving door on their rap sheets, but more often than not merely petty criminals, or even just the troubled, the substance addicted, or the mentally disturbed. This makes America's indifference to this problem that much more tragic.

Until a bomb exploded in New York's World Trade Center in 1993, we could only remotely identify with the terror that grips the citizens of Belfast or Israel or Sarajevo, or those unfortunates who died or were maimed in Iraq during the Gulf War. Only when the Long Island Railroad's 5:33 was turned into a death train by a crazed gunman named Colin Ferguson in 1993 did white suburbanites across the country realize that they could run but not hide from the threat of urban crime

> *"Good police officers have little to fear from proper administrative handling of excessive force complaints."*

and violence. Only then did some measure of gun control legislation pass Congress for the first time in over a quarter century—by a hair's breadth. What was curious about the Long Island tragedy was the fact that public officials who had not supported strengthening the penalties for bias-related crimes were among the first to seek prosecution of Colin Ferguson under those same statutes.

To paraphrase Malcolm X, America's chickens were coming home to roost as the century drew to a close, and not one by one but in droves. Yet the message was still not clear. The death of Shuaib Latif [a 17-year-old black Muslim who was shot and killed by police in a dark basement in 1994] in Brooklyn took a side stage in the media to the posturing and posing of black activist Al Sharpton, whose name was easier for reporters to spell and pronounce than those adopted by the imams of Al Amin Abdul Latif's mosque.

Quick Fixes

America's focus on violent crime is currently blurred by its fascination with quick fixes; witness the popularity of the latest criminal justice catchphrase, "three strikes and you're out." Legislators pass more laws for more people to break, which will require the building of more jails which are nothing more than universities for crime in their current form. The requisite focus on poverty, unemployment, crumbling school systems, and deficiencies in child care, let alone on police brutality, is anything but popular. New York City has elected a mayor [Rudolph Giuliani] who seems intent on undermining its community policing program, one of the few positive changes in law enforcement to take place there in years. And one of the first salvos against crime fired by Rudolph Giuliani was aimed straight at a helpless underclass, when he pushed for criminalization of the homeless, with an emphasis on locking up squeegee-wielding panhandlers.

Most Americans would rather not hear the cries of police brutality victims, and choose to deny the pervasiveness of such abuse of power unless they can view it on videotape. Apologists argue that the police have a hard enough job as it is without unnecessarily dwelling on their deficiencies. What the apologists have yet to realize is that cops who use deadly force indiscriminately make the job of good cops even harder yet. Such drum beating and mindless simplicity should not be surprising, however, at a time in our history when Rush Limbaugh and Howard Stern make it to the bestseller list, when television news shows are dominated by sensational tabloid stories such as the Bobbitt dismemberment and the exploits of Joey Buttafuoco and Amy Fisher. [Lorena Bobbitt was convicted of malicious wounding for cutting off her husband's penis with a kitchen knife in 1993. Amy Fisher, 17, was convicted of attempted murder for trying to kill the wife of her 38-year-old lover, Joey Buttafuoco, in 1992.]

"People Like Us"

If Americans were truly interested in addressing the deadly force issue, then the legislation proposed while the King case and its violent aftermath was still fresh in everyone's minds would have passed in one form or another. But there was no continuing public outcry from our country's dominant white middle class—because beatings like King's don't happen "to people like us."

There is an Italian-American high school student in the Bensonhurst section of Brooklyn who feels differently. In 1993, this young man, the star of his school's football team, got into a fight with another student. A beat cop broke up the fracas, and in the process assaulted the football star.

"You make a complaint about this," the cop said, "And I will arrest you."

The football star told his parents, who took him with them to the Bath Avenue stationhouse, toting along some heavy baggage of righteous indignation. They were told to wait. True to his word, the officer then arrested the youth; after this, their complaints fell on deaf ears. The initial beating was compounded by an abuse of authority that the parents thought could never be used against people like them.

> *"A nation of laws cannot and should not elevate anyone above the law—not ourselves, not the president of the country, and not the cop on the beat."*

Norman Siegel, director of the New York Civil Liberties Union, agreed to review the case. . . . The parents said that they never thought they would seek the help of the NYCLU, which until they needed it was definitely *not* on their list of favorite charities. How many more working-class, nonminority young men will have to be abused by police before their parents are stripped of their smug sense of security, and realize that excessive use of force and abuse of authority is their problem too?

Demanding Accountability from the Highest Levels

As for the police themselves, it is highly unlikely that the majority of officers in this country who read the horror stories will react with anything but revulsion—especially to the paucity of accountability demanded by the official response. Good police officers have little to fear from proper administrative handling of excessive force complaints; if a more open attitude is taken, then those who are truly innocent of anything they could be charged with will benefit as well.

A nation of laws cannot and should not elevate anyone above the law—not ourselves, not the president of the country, and not the cop on the beat. Only when we seek justice for justice's sake, rather than weakly permit it to be effected in order to avoid the next riotous outburst, can we truly call our society worthy of being spared the wages of someone's next sins.

Until a system exists that demands accountability at the highest levels for police actions that result in needless death, with an open, public forum as the venue for the fact-finding process, the credibility of our entire system of justice will exist under an ominous shadow of mistrust and doubt.

Congressional Oversight of Federal Law Enforcement Agencies Would Reduce Brutality

by Robert J. Caldwell

About the author: *Robert J. Caldwell is the editor of the Sunday editorial section of the* San Diego Union-Tribune *newspaper.*

No cause is well served by zealots or fanatics, and least of all by terrorists.

Accordingly, legitimate questions about misconduct by federal law enforcement agencies have been clouded by the tragic terrorist bombing in Oklahoma City, by the unsettling militia movement and by such diversionary tempests as that prompted by the rhetorical excesses of the National Rifle Association.

It hardly needs repeating that the criminals responsible for the bombing that killed 169 men, women and children in the Murrah Federal Office Building in Oklahoma City must be caught, tried, convicted and then punished to the maximum extent of the law.

It's equally obvious that armed, paramilitary groups are a disturbing phenomenon and, perhaps, a potential threat to public safety in some instances. If the latter, they need monitoring by the appropriate authorities.

And, of course, shrill rhetoric from the NRA, prompting another round of sometimes equally shrill NRA bashing from the press and the Clinton White House, adds nothing useful to public discourse on the issue in question.

That issue, simply put, is whether certain federal law enforcement agencies including the Bureau of Alcohol, Tobacco and Firearms (BATF), the FBI and the Drug Enforcement Administration (DEA) have been guilty of running roughshod over the citizenry they are pledged to serve and protect.

The short answer, abundantly supported by the evidence, certainly appears to be, yes.

Reprinted from Robert J. Caldwell, "'Jack-Booted Government Thugs' Goes Too Far, but . . . ," *San Diego Union-Tribune*, June 4, 1995, p. G-1. Reprinted with permission from the *San Diego Union-Tribune*.

One need not be a militia member drilling in the woods with a Kalashnikov to reach this conclusion. Indeed, it is shared by more than a few members of Congress, by civil liberties groups, and, if the latest polls are any indication, by a sizable portion of the American people.

Exhibit one is the Waco debacle. There, on April 19, 1993, an FBI-BATF assault led by armored vehicles fitted with battering rams and spraying potent CS riot gas precipitated the deaths of 80 or more religious cultists barricaded in their rural compound. Among the dead were more than a dozen children who couldn't have been guilty of any crime.

The Justice Department insists the cultists, led by the messianic and possibly deranged David Koresh, set the fires that consumed them as fulfillment of Koresh's apocalyptic vision. Maybe so, although there is at least some evidence to the contrary.

In any case, even Attorney General Janet Reno, who accepted responsibility for ordering the attack, acknowledges the obvious: that, in retrospect, the assault was a tragic blunder. But Reno vigorously disputes any suggestion that the federal government was in any way responsible for the slaughter of the Branch Davidians.

> *"Federal law enforcement agencies . . . have been guilty of running roughshod over the citizenry they are pledged to serve and protect."*

Others are less forgiving. Harvard professor Alan Stone, a psychiatrist brought in by the Justice Department to advise the FBI during the long siege that preceded the final assault, says federal agents consistently rejected advice that might have defused the standoff and precluded its ghastly end.

The botched BATF raid that led to the Waco siege was itself a stunning example of incompetence compounded by the bureau's Rambo-like mentality.

Koresh and his mind-controlled Branch Davidians were suspected of illegally possessing automatic weapons. Koresh could have been arrested easily enough during his occasional trips into Waco. A search warrant might then have been served peacefully on his sheep-like flock at the compound. Instead, heavily armed BATF agents went ahead with a paramilitary assault on the Davidian compound despite *knowing* that Koresh and his armed followers had learned of the pending attack and were prepared to defend themselves.

The predictable, and entirely preventable, result was a deadly shootout in which four BATF agents and several Davidians were killed and more on both sides were wounded. Next came the siege and, in time, the conflagration that consumed the many innocent along with the few guilty.

If the Waco disaster were the only example of federal law enforcement run amok, there would be less cause for concern. But it isn't.

In 1992, an undercover BATF agent induced Idaho white separatist Randy Weaver to sell him two illegally sawed-off shotguns. When Weaver subsequently failed to make a court date, federal marshals went to his forest cabin. In the ensuing altercation, the marshals fatally shot Weaver's teen-aged son in the back. A marshal was then shot, reportedly in self-defense, by a Weaver family friend. The FBI promptly dispatched sniper teams to the siege of Weaver's cabin.

An FBI sniper shot Weaver in the back and then killed his unarmed wife with a bullet through the head while she was holding their 10-month-old baby. A jury exonerated Randy Weaver on the shotgun charge, ruling that he had been illegally entrapped by the government. Federal Judge Edward Lodge strongly rebuked the government, declaring that the FBI's conduct constituted a "callous disregard for the rights of the defendants and the interests of justice."

And there is more, including a San Diego case for which the federal government is still ducking full accountability.

In August, 1992, heavily armed Drug Enforcement Administration and U.S. Customs Service agents, acting on a spurious tip by a drug informant known to be unreliable, burst into Donald Carlson's home in Poway just after midnight. A frightened Carlson, his home under attack and invaded in the dark by persons unknown, grabbed a pistol to defend himself. Federal agents then shot him three times (once in the back when he was already prostrate on the floor), inflicting wounds that kept Carlson hospitalized for months and caused permanent disability.

No drugs were found. Carlson, a businessman with no criminal record, sued the government and won a sizable compensatory judgment.

But he was nearly killed. And no one in the DEA or Customs has been held accountable for this outrageous, almost fatal assault on the home and person of a law-abiding citizen.

In February, 1993, eight BATF agents kicked in the door of Janet Hart's home in Portland, Ore. and then ransacked her house looking for evidence of cocaine trafficking and illegal firearms sales. Only after she had been rudely interrogated in the presence of her children and then arrested and taken in for booking was it discovered, by the Portland police, that the DEA had the wrong name and the wrong person.

> *"Congress . . . [must] demand that those responsible [for law enforcement misconduct and misjudgments] be held fully accountable."*

DEA agents looking for drugs battered down the door of a Guthrie, Okla. man's home in 1991. The agents handcuffed and kicked the man in front of his wife and daughters, then realized that they had the wrong address. Reportedly, they left without apologizing.

In September, 1991, a small army of armed agents from the DEA, BATF, and the U.S. Forest Service staged a nighttime raid on the home of Sina Brush in Montairnair, N.M. Brush and her daughters, clad only in their underwear, were handcuffed and interrogated on their knees while the house was searched. No drugs were found. The search warrant had been based on faulty information provided by an unreliable informant.

The National Rifle Association, in its now celebrated fund-raising letter, called these and other abuses by federal law enforcement agencies evidence of "jack-booted government thugs." That was too sweeping an indictment by an organization whose bare-knuckled tactics and inflammatory rhetoric are hurting the cause of lawful gun ownership.

But, clearly, there is a disturbing pattern here; a documented record of abuses that raise serious questions about the conduct and accountability of federal law enforcement agencies. The Justice Department's stubborn state of denial on Waco and the Weaver case demonstrate that the Clinton administration remains part of the problem. Wrist-slap reprimands for FBI supervisors and reshuffling the BATF leadership do not atone for misconduct and misjudgments that cost the lives of innocent people.

That leaves it up to Congress to begin exercising its oversight responsibility for federal law enforcement. A searching congressional inquiry into the Waco tragedy is essential, and long overdue. So is a wider review by the appropriate congressional committees of other federal law enforcement abuses. For starters, Congress could do what Clinton, Reno and company won't; demand that those responsible be held fully accountable.

Communities Must Stand Up to the Police

by Van Jones

About the author: *Van Jones is the director of the Ella Baker Center for Human Rights in San Francisco.*

Looking to make an example of someone, security forces enter a middle-income neighborhood. Two officers single out a youth for arrest, pick him up and slam him viciously on the pavement. His mother emerges from her home, screaming "My baby! My baby! Stop!" One officer spins around and punches the woman in the stomach, doubling her over.

Seeing this, hundreds of people come pouring out of their houses. They free the boy, rough up the officers and send them on their way. Sirens wailing and lights flashing, the security forces return minutes later intent on restoring order. But the growing crowd—made up of mamas and grandmamas and every-day folks—refuses to retreat, facing off with their tormentors and declaring, "You can't come in this neighborhood beating on our children anymore."

Thrilling stuff, huh? A scene from Northern Ireland? Palestine? Apartheid South Africa? A new Hollywood release? The answer: None of the above. This all happened in San Francisco's Potrero Hill neighborhood—on January 9, 1997.

The incident was not isolated. Just a few weeks before, residents of St. Petersburg, Florida, had taken to the streets after police killed an unarmed man.

Rebellions Against Exploitation and Oppression

Under ordinary circumstances, uprisings like these are almost unheard of. Most sane people avoid challenging cops, even verbally. But let me make a bold prediction: By the end of 1997, similar acts of mass resistance will have occurred in nearly every major U.S. city.

These mini-rebellions will not be the result of urban Zapatistas organizing for a conscious insurrection against exploitation and oppression. Instead, they will occur because police officers will be pushing around increasingly desperate

Reprinted from Van Jones, "Battling Police State USA," *Third Force*, March/April 1997, by permission of the Center for Third World Organizing.

people for increasingly stupid reasons. And folks simply won't be havin' it.

You can see it coming. Unequal societies maintain "order" in two ways: with the carrot of social aid and opportunity programs, and with the stick of tough laws, mean cops and waiting jails. As the government dices up the carrot (by cutting welfare, eliminating affirmative action, etc.), it must necessarily use more of the stick. The welfare state shrinks; the police state grows.

Recipe for Disaster

That process is well under way. The Prison Activist Resource Center reports that in 1980, the federal government spent $27 billion on elementary and secondary education and job training programs combined, and only $8 billion on prisons. By 1995, that $27 billion had plunged to $16 billion, while spending on "corrections" had skyrocketed to a whopping $20 billion per year!

It's a recipe for disaster. Take "less help," add "more cops" and shake: Boom.

History suggests that episodes of police abuse or murder will trigger the explosions. Our challenge as organizers is to figure out ways to steer the rage into sustained strategic campaigns for concrete police reforms. Through those fights, we must build lasting organizations that can win concessions from police departments and challenge the politicians who value cops over teachers, jails over day care centers, and tough laws over decent social programs. In this way, we can lay the groundwork for a people's movement with the moral authority and political momentum to make sweeping changes in society as a whole.

We don't need to change the whole thing at once to make a big difference. But we can still fight for—and win—meaningful reforms to reduce that violence by strengthening civilian oversight, banning lethal weapons like pepper spray, and calling for the removal of abusive officers and killer cops.

Police reform fights can be an arena in which people of color, sexual minorities, low-income people, youth and union activists can fight side by side, learning to work together to build collective power.

Sound like a pipe dream? I have

> *"[These mini-rebellions] will occur because police officers will be pushing around increasingly desperate people. . . . And folks simply won't be havin' it."*

seen the future in Fairfield, California. There, an African American family whose son was wrongly arrested and beaten by the police called a house meeting of concerned neighbors. Within a month, a diverse assortment of community members had developed a campaign to clean up the police department.

If people across the country start organizing in this way, then I'd be willing to make another prediction: That it won't be long before ordinary people—by the thousands and by the millions—come out of their houses to stand with their neighbors. Not to rescue another mother and child, but to protect and secure a future for all mothers and all children everywhere.

Bibliography

Books

Amnesty International USA   *Police Brutality and Excessive Force in the New York City Police Department.* New York: Amnesty International USA, 1996.

Lou Cannon   *Official Negligence: How Rodney King and the Riots Changed Los Angeles and the LAPD.* New York: Times Books, 1998.

Paul Chevigny   *Edge of the Knife: Police Violence in the Americas.* New York: New Press, 1995.

Edwin J. Delattre and Patrick V. Murphy   *Character and Cops: Ethics in Policing.* Washington, DC: American Enterprise Institute for Public Policy Research, 1996.

John DeSantis   *The New Untouchables: How America Sanctions Police Violence.* Chicago: Noble Press, 1994.

Joe Domanick   *To Protect and to Serve: The LAPD's Century of War in the City of Dreams.* New York: Pocket Books, 1994.

Joel Garner   *Understanding the Use of Force by and Against the Police.* Washington, DC: U.S. Department of Justice, 1996.

George L. Kelling and Catherine M. Coles   *Fixing Broken Windows: Restoring Order and Reducing Crime in Our Communities.* New York: Martin Kessler Books, 1996.

Rickey D. Lashley   *Policework: The Need for a Noble Character.* Westport, CT: Praeger, 1995.

Tom McEwen   *National Data Collection on Police Use of Force.* Washington, DC: National Institute of Justice, 1996.

Maryann Miller   *Everything You Need to Know About Dealing with the Police.* New York: Rosen, 1995.

Elijah Muhammad   *Police Brutality.* Atlanta: Secretarius, 1997.

160

Bibliography

National Association for the Advancement of Colored People
Beyond the Rodney King Story: An Investigation of Police Conduct in Minority Communities. Boston: Northeastern University Press, 1995.

Roberto Rodriguez
Justice: A Question of Race. Tempe, AZ: Bilingual Press, 1997.

Walter Edward Schultz
Police—Health, Risks, Shift Work, Attitudes, and Brutality Force: Index of New Information. Washington, DC: ABBE, 1995.

Ellen M. Scrivner
The Role of Police Psychology in Controlling Excessive Force. Washington, DC: U.S. Department of Justice, 1994.

Jerome H. Skolnick and James J. Fyfe
Above the Law: Police and the Excessive Use of Force. New York: Free Press, 1993.

Samuel Walker, Cassia Spohn, and Miriam DeLone
The Color of Justice: Race, Ethnicity, and Crime in America. Belmont, CA: Wadsworth, 1996.

Linn Washington
Beating Goes On: Police Brutality in America. Monroe, ME: Common Courage, 1998.

Periodicals

Mumia Abu-Jamal
"War Crimes," *Plough,* October 1997. Available from Spring Valley Brudenhof, Farmington, PA 15437-9506.

John Anner
"Community Safety and Police Accountability," *Z Magazine,* July/August 1995.

Brinton E. Bohling
"Public Employer Liability," *Monthly Labor Review,* October 1997.

Angela Bonavoglia
"Breaking the Blue Wall of Silence," *Ms.,* January/February 1997.

William Booth
"Taking a Bigger SWAT at Crime," *Washington Post National Weekly Edition,* June 30, 1997. Available from 1150 15th St. NW, Washington, DC 20071.

Fred Bruning
"Rogue Cops and Civilian Beatings," *Maclean's,* April 29, 1996.

Alexander Cockburn
"Free Radio, Crazy Cops, and Broken Windows," *Nation,* December 15, 1997.

Francis T. Cullen et al.
"Stop or I'll Shoot: Racial Differences in Support for Police Use of Deadly Force," *American Behavioral Scientist,* February 1996.

Susan Douglas
"The Making of a Bully," *Progressive,* October 1997.

Michael Ervin
"A Memorial for Stolen Lives," *Progressive,* December 1997.

Christopher John Farley
"A Beating in Brooklyn," *Time,* August 25, 1997.

Michael A. Fletcher   "May the Driver Beware," *Washington Post National Weekly Edition,* April 8–14, 1996.

David Gergen   "A War We've Begun to Win," *U.S. News & World Report,* June 16, 1997.

Elizabeth Gleick   "The Crooked Blue Line," *Time,* September 11, 1995.

Bob Herbert   "A Cop's View," *New York Times,* March 15, 1998.

Bob Herbert   "Reprise of Terror," *New York Times,* March 12, 1998.

David Kocieniewski   "System of Policing the Police Is Attacked from Without and Within," *New York Times,* December 19, 1997.

James Lardner   "A Mythical Blue Wall of Silence," *U.S. News & World Report,* September 1, 1997.

Charles Mahtesian   "The Big Blue Hiring Spree," *Governing,* January 1996.

Yohance Maqubela   "NYPD Strategy Number 9," *City Limits,* February 1997.

Mike McAlary   "The Last Cop Story," *Esquire,* December 1997.

Joseph D. McNamara   "A Veteran Chief: Too Many Cops Think It's a War," *Time,* September 1, 1997.

Thomas Fields Meyer   "Under Suspicion," *People Weekly,* January 15, 1996.

Chris Mitchell   "The Brutal Truth," *City Limits,* December 1997.

New Republic   "Bad Cop, Good Cops," September 8–15, 1997.

Christian Parenti   "Police Crime," *Z Magazine,* March 1996.

Richard Rayner   "Wanted: A Kinder, Gentler Cop," *New York Times Magazine,* January 22, 1995.

Larry Reibstein   "NYPD Black and Blue," *Newsweek,* June 2, 1997.

William F. Schulz   "Cruel and Unusual Punishment," *New York Review of Books,* April 24, 1997.

Bruce Shapiro   "Policing Brutality," *Nation,* September 22, 1997.

Bruce Shapiro   "When Justice Kills," *Nation,* June 9, 1997.

Jeffery T. Walker   "Police and Correctional Use of Force: Legal and Policy Standards and Implications," *Crime & Delinquency,* January 1996.

Lynne Wilson   "Pepper Spray Madness," *CovertAction Quarterly,* Spring 1996.

Mike Zielinski   "Armed and Dangerous: Private Police on the March," *CovertAction Quarterly,* Fall 1995.

Organizations to Contact

The editors have compiled the following list of organizations concerned with the issues debated in this book. The descriptions are derived from materials provided by the organizations. All have publications or information available for interested readers. The list was compiled on the date of publication of the present volume; the information provided here may change. Be aware that many organizations take several weeks or longer to respond to inquiries, so allow as much time as possible.

American Civil Liberties Union (ACLU)
132 W. 43rd St., New York, NY 10036
(212) 944-9800 • fax: (212) 869-9065
e-mail: aclu@aclu.org • website: http://www.aclu.org

The ACLU is a national organization that works to defend Americans' civil rights guaranteed in the U.S. Constitution. Among other services, the ACLU provides legal assistance to victims of police abuse. The ACLU publishes *Fighting Police Abuse: A Community Action Manual* as well as the semiannual newsletter *Civil Liberties Alert.*

Amnesty International (AI)
322 Eighth Ave., New York, NY 10001
(212) 807-8400
e-mail: admin-us@aiusa.org
websites: http://www.amnesty.org • http://www.amnesty-usa.org

Amnesty International is a worldwide campaigning movement that works to promote human rights and opposes cruel treatment of prisoners. Its 1996 report *Police Brutality and Excessive Force in the New York City Police Department* is available on the AI website.

International Association of Chiefs of Police
515 N. Washington St., Alexandria, VA 22314
(703) 836-6767 • (800) THE IACP • fax: (703) 836-4543
website: http://www.theiacp.org

The association consists of police executives who provide consultation and research services to, and support educational programs for, police departments nationwide. The association publishes *Police Chief* magazine monthly, which covers all aspects of law enforcement duty.

National Association for the Advancement of Colored People (NAACP)
4805 Mt. Hope Dr., Baltimore, MD 21215-3297
(410) 358-9000 • fax: (410) 358-3818
information hot line: (410) 521-4939
website: http://www.naacp.org

The NAACP is a civil rights organization that works to end racial discrimination in America. It researches and documents police brutality and provides legal services for victims of brutality. The NAACP publishes the book *Beyond the Rodney King Story: An Investigation of Police Misconduct in Minority Communities,* the magazine *Crisis* ten times per year, and *Police-Citizen Violence: An Organizing Guide for Community Leaders,* which is available from its civil rights archives.

National Institute of Justice (NIJ)
National Criminal Justice Reference Service (NCJRS)
PO Box 6000, Rockville, MD 20850
(800) 851-3420 • (301) 519-5500
e-mail: askncjrs@ncjrs.org • website: http://www.ojp.usdoj.gov/nij

A component of the Office of Justice Programs of the U.S. Department of Justice, NIJ supports and conducts research on crime, criminal behavior, and crime prevention. NCJRS acts as a clearinghouse for criminal justice information for researchers and other interested individuals. It publishes and distributes the following reports from the Bureau of Justice Statistics: *National Data Collection on Police Use of Force, The Role of Psychology in Controlling Excessive Force,* and *Understanding the Use of Force by and Against the Police.*

National Organization of Black Law Enforcement Executives (NOBLE)
4609 Pinecrest Office Park Dr., Suite F, Alexandria, VA 22312-1442
(703) 658-1529 • fax: (703) 658-9479
e-mail: noble@noblenatl.org • website: http://www.noblenatl.org

NOBLE serves the interests of black law enforcement officials. It works to eliminate racism, increase minority participation at all levels of law enforcement, and foster community involvement in working to reduce urban crime and violence. NOBLE condemns the use of excessive force by police. Its publications include the quarterly magazine *NOBLE National* and the newsletter *NOBLE Actions.*

October 22nd Coalition
c/o KHL, Inc., PO Box 124, 160 First Ave., New York, NY 10009
(888) No-Brutality • NYC: (212) 822-8596 • Chicago: (773) 794-8114
e-mail: oct22@unstoppable.com • website: http://www.unstoppable.com/22

The coalition is a diverse group of activist organizations and individuals concerned about police brutality. October 22nd is the date of the coalition's annual "National Day of Protest Against Police Brutality, Repression, and the Criminalization of a Generation," which is intended to raise awareness about police misconduct. The coalition publishes a newsletter, available on-line, as part of its efforts to organize protest activities. It also coordinates the *Stolen Lives Project,* a report that documents the names of those who have been brutalized and killed by the police since 1990.

People Against Racial Terror (PART)
PO Box 1055, Culver City, CA 90232
(310) 288-5003
e-mail: part2001@usa.net • website: http://www.geocities.com/CapitolHill/Lobby/4801

PART believes that police abuse, brutality, and corruption are widespread problems that demand immediate national attention. PART views the police as an occupying army in oppressed communities, and it believes community monitoring of police is the best way to prevent incidents of police harassment and violence. In addition to books and videos, PART publishes *Turning the Tide: Journal of Anti-Racist Activism, Research, and Education.*

Police Executive Research Forum (PERF)
1120 Connecticut Ave. NW, Suite 930, Washington, DC 20036
(202) 466-7820
website: http://www.policeforum.org

PERF is a national professional association of police executives that seeks to increase public understanding of and stimulate debate on important criminal justice issues. PERF's numerous publications include the book *And Justice for All: Understanding and Controlling Police Abuse of Force* and the papers *The Force Factor: Measuring Police Use of Force Relative to Suspect Resistance* and *Police Use of Force: A Statistical Analysis of the Metro-Dade Police Department.*

Police Foundation
1201 Connecticut Ave. NW, Suite 200, Washington, DC 20036
(202) 833-1460 • fax: (202) 659-9149
e-mail: pfinfo@policefoundation.org

The foundation conducts research projects on police practices and aims to improve the quality of police personnel. It publishes the report *Officer Behavior in Police-Citizen Encounters: A Descriptive Model and Implications for Less-Than-Lethal Alternatives* and the book *Police Use of Force: Official Reports, Citizen Complaints, and Legal Consequences.*

Index

ABC *World News Tonight,* 37
Above the Law (Skolnick and Fyfe), 70, 84
African Americans
  complaints of brutality registered by, 141
  police credibility among, 87
  police harassment of, 90, 91–92, 104–106
  as police officers
    brutality by, 80
    recruitment of, 60, 137–38
  views of police, 133–34
Alcivar, Lenny, 73
American Civil Liberties Union, 117
American Friends Service Committee, 26
  responses to complaints filed by, 28
Amnesty International, 17
Arias, Raymond, 75
Arroyo, Abel, 27
assertive/aggressive policing
  is not cause of police brutality, 141–42
  theory behind, 73
  see also zero tolerance strategy

Baez, Anthony, 25, 66
Baird, John, 131
Barry, Dan, 64
Becker, Gregory, 59–60
Berkeley, California
  citizen oversight of police in, 122
Beyond 911 (Sparrow et al.), 138–39
Biden, Joseph, 127
Black, Donald, 78
Blackman, Paul H., 22
Bobb, Merrick, 69
Bobbitt, Lorena, 152
Branch Davidians, 21, 149, 155–56
Bratton, William, 19, 39, 48, 50, 74
Brush, Sina, 157
brutality
  by federal agents
    congressional oversight would reduce,
      154–57
    is serious problem, 21–23
  by police
    assertive policing contributes to, 72–75

incidents of, 24–25, 66–68, 90, 91–92,
  112, 158
  is serious problem, 17–20
    con, 39–40
  against Hispanics, 26–29
  against illegal immigrants, 44–47
  against minorities, 24–25, 75
  leads to loss of trust, 98–100
  media reporting of
    is downplayed, 36–38
    is incomplete, 52–54
    is overemphasized, 55–56
  officer inexperience is main cause, 40,
    74
  police attitudes contribute to, 76–79
  prevention of
    overview, 108–11
    radical changes are needed for,
      112–16
    should not hinder effective crime
      control, 48–51
  racism is cause of, 59–63
  reveals injustice of capitalism, 84–88
  against prisoners, is serious problem,
    30–39
Bryant, James, 30

Caldwell, Robert J., 154
Campbell, David Scott, 34
Cannon, Lou, 46
capitalism
  police brutality reveals injustice of,
    84–88
Carlson, Donald, 156
Carrillo, Karen, 30
Cauchon, Dennis, 72
Cedeno, Kevin, 142
Chaney, Ben, 30, 33
Chaney, James Earl, 32
Chase, John, 27
Chevigny, Paul, 67, 78
Chicago Citizen, 80
Christopher Commission, 63
  on police accountability, 136

166

Index

Civilian Complaint Review Board (New York City)
  complaints to, are declining, 40
    con, 18–19
civilian review boards/systems
  definition of, 118–19
  importance of, 119
  must police police, 124–32
  police hostility toward, 125–26
  principles for effectiveness of, 119–20
  stages of union resistance to, 128
civil lawsuits
  for police misconduct, 17–18
Clinton, Bill, 149
Commission of Human Rights Abuse in Mississippi, 34
communities
  must stand up to police, 158–59
  oversight by
    police should be subject to, 117–23
  police involvement in, is needed, 133–39
  police residency in, 147
  policing by, 62–63
    need for, in black communities, 138–39
complaints, civilian
  by African Americans, 141
  are declining, 40
    because victims are giving up, 108
    con, 18–19
  are imprecise measure of police misconduct, 75
  few result in disciplinary action, 72
  to INS, 27
    responses to, 28
  in New York, rise in, 141
  in Philadelphia, internal review of, 131
Constitution, U.S.
  provision for federal policing in, 22
Corry, John, 44
Costello, Rich, 124
Crew, John, 127–28
Cronkite, Walter, 45

Dark Journey: Black Mississippians in the Age of Jim Crow (McMillen), 32
Davis, Len, 110
DeSantis, John, 148
DiCoscia, Nancy, 75
Dinkins, David N., 50, 75, 99, 111, 140
Dominguez, Edward, 66, 70–71
Dowd, Michael, 124
Doyle, Megan, 68
drug war
  has militarized federal law enforcement, 22

Evans, Paul, 110

Farmer, Catherine M., 21
Farrakhan, Louis, 33
Fazlollah, Mark, 131
federal agents/agencies
  brutality by
    congressional oversight would reduce, 154–57
    is serious problem, 21–23
Ferguson, Colin, 151
Fernandez, Vicente, 70–71
Final Call (periodical), 33
Finnegan, Lawrence J., Jr., 98
Fisher, Amy, 152
Florez, Enrique Nunez, 44–45, 46
force, extreme
  use is sometimes justified, 41
Ford, Nancy L., 52
François, Donatien Alphonse. *See* Sade, Marquis de
Fuhrman, Mark, 59
Fyfe, James J., 70, 76, 84

Gammage, Jonny, 24, 41, 104, 109–10
Geller, William, 60, 63
Gibbs, Andrea, 35
Gilmore, Brian, 102
Giuliani, Rudolph, 37, 48, 65, 73, 111, 151
  reform is not priority of, 145–46
  response to Abner Louima assault, 140
  response to police misconduct, 142–43
Goodman, Andrew, 32
Gould, Joseph, 59
Gutierrez, Jose Antonio, 37

Hagan, Dianne Liuzzi, 104
Hampton, Ronald, 62, 81
Harris, Taquana, 64
Hart, Janet, 156
Henderson, Keith, 41
Higgins, Stephen, 22
Hikind, Doy, 70
Hill, Patricia, 60
Hispanics
  as illegal immigrants, police brutality against is exaggerated, 44–47
  police brutality against is serious problem, 26–29
Holland v. O'Brien, 102
Huspek, Michael, 26
Hynes, Charles, 149

illegal immigrants
  police brutality against is exaggerated, 44–47

Immigration and Naturalization Service
(INS), 27
Indianapolis
citizen oversight in, 120
Ingram, Jim, 34

Jackson, Bernice Powell, 24
Jackson, Jesse, 41
Jackson, Sherman, 75
Jackson Advocate, 32–33
James Earl Chaney Foundation, 34
Johnson, Terrence, 101–102
Jones, Andre Lamond, 30, 33
Jones, Van, 158
Jones-Quinn, Esther, 30, 33

Kane, George, 84
Kelling, George, 48, 73, 111
Kelly, Raymond, 144
Kennedy, Joseph C., 89
King, Rodney G. *See* Rodney King case
Kluge, Charles, 127
Kopel, David, 22
Koresh, David, 155
Koshetz, Rae Dawn, 71
Ku Klux Klan, 32

Lacayo, Richard, 108
Latif, Shuaib, 151
Latinos. *See* Hispanics
Livoti, Francis X., 66
London, Stuart, 66, 67
Los Angeles
reports of police brutality in, 87
Los Angeles Times, 45, 87
Louima, Abner, assault on, 39, 40, 48, 51,
66, 72
Mayor Giuliani's response to, 140
media overdid reporting of, 55–56
original charge against, 73
as sadistic, 98, 99, 100, 108
was no aberration, 112

McCabe, Gerald, 124
McCarthy, Sarah J., 41
McDonald, Valerie, 43
McMillen, Neil R., 32
Minneapolis
reports of police brutality in, 87
minorities
police brutality against is serious
problem, 24–25, 75
Mississippi Freedom Summer, 32, 35
Mollen Commission, 19, 99
proposals of, 144–45

Muwakkil, Salim, 59
National Association for the Advancement
of Colored People, 133
National Coalition on Police Accountability, 116, 125
National Law Enforcement Officer Rights
Center, 127
National Rifle Association, 157
Neuman, Jon O., 150
New Orleans
police reforms in, 110
news media
exaggerates violence against illegal
immigrants, 45–46
reporting of police brutality
is downplayed, 36–38
is incomplete, 52–54
is overemphasized, 55–56
New York City
decline in murder rate in, 48
focus on disorder crimes in, 49–51
has increased police misconduct cases,
65–66
police misconduct in
has increased, 65–66
Mayor Giuliani's response to, 141–42
proposals to end, 144–45
as related to police corruption, 145
70th precinct, 73–75
New York Times, 24, 46, 130

O'Brien, Timothy, 109
October 22nd Coalition to Stop Police
Brutality, 116
O'Keefe, James, 68
Oklahoma City bombing, 23, 154

Parks, Bernard, 109
Peel, Robert, 84
Pelayo, Henry, 70–71
Pennington, Richard, 110
People Against Racist Terror, 112
points of action proposed by,
113–16
Pérez, Edith, 109
Perkins, Joseph, 47
Philadelphia
citizen oversight committee in, 124
police resistance to citizen review in,
130–32
police/policing
assertive, contributes to police brutality,
72–75
attitudes of, contribute to police brutality,
76–79

black, recruitment of, 60
brutality
    leads to loss of trust in, 98–100
    makes citizens feel less safe, 104–106
    prosecution under RICO Act, 150
    public officials must denounce, 140–47
    relationship with police corruption, 145
    results in loss of respect in, 101–103
    can abuse power to arrest, 68–70
    can overreact to challenges to authority,
        64–71
    categorization of citizens by, 77–78
    civilian review boards must police,
        124–32
    code of silence among, 81, 99, 110, 125
    culture of, contributes to police brutality,
        80–81
    deaths caused by, are increasing, 19–20
    is relatively new institution, 84
    need community involvement, 133–39
    need for accountability of, 136–37,
        148–53
    policy, community oversight of, 122
    responding to crime vs. preserving social
        order, 86–87
    rookie officers are main cause of
        brutality, 40, 74
    shootings, community control of, 121
    should be subject to community
        oversight, 115–16, 117–23
    typical recruit, 76
    unions, 126–27
        lobbying by, 129
        resistance to citizen review by, 127–28
Powell, Colin, 43
President's Commission on Law
    Enforcement and Administration of
    Justice, 78
Prison Activist Resource Center, 159
prisoners
    brutality against is serious problem,
        30–39

racism
    is cause of police brutality, 59–63
    toward whites, 42–43
Racketeer Influenced Corrupt Organiza-
    tions Act (RICO)
    use to prosecute police brutality, 150
Reiss, Albert, Jr., 78
Reno, Janet, 149
Revolutionary Worker, 36
Rhodes, Nancy, 130
RICO, 150
Rizzo, Frank, 60

Roberts, Paul Craig, 21
Roberts, Richard, 140
Rodney King case, 63, 79
    changes in social climate following, 148
    media reports of, were incomplete, 52–54
    was no aberration, 61
Rodriguez, Francisco, 70, 71
Rosenbaum, Yankel, 149, 150
Royko, Mike, 61
Ruby Ridge incident, 21

Sacco and Vanzetti case, 116
Sade, Marquis de, 98, 100
San Francisco
    citizen oversight in, 123
Sarid, Sahar, 69, 70
Schwerner, Michael, 32
Seals, Ray, 25, 41, 104
Seattle Police Officers Guild, 128
Seymore, Lesley, 61
Sharpton, Al, 151
Siegel, Norman, 73, 108, 152
Sierra, Jose, Jr., 72, 75
Simpson, O.J., 87
Sistrunk, Dicky, 34
Skogan, Wesley, 51
Skolnick, Jerome H., 70, 76, 84
Snyder, Douglas, 66, 68
Sobran, Joseph, 55
Sontag, Deborah, 64
Sparrow, Malcolm K., 138
Spokane
    police resistance to citizen review in, 130
Stone, Alan, 155
Summers, Clyde W., 129

Taylor, Adama, 42
Terry v. Ohio, 141
Till, Emmett, 32
Time magazine, 37
Tisdale, Charles, 32, 33
Tong, Nancy, 66, 67
Tucson
    citizen oversight in, 123

unions, police
    lobbying by, 129
    resistance to civilian oversight,
        127–28
    vs. traditional labor unions, 126

Van Maanen, John, 77

Waco siege. *See* Branch Davidians
Waddell, Glenn, 34

Walker, Cedric, 30–31
Walker Report, 87
Wall Street Journal, 60
Washington Afro-American, 101
Washington Post, 46
Washington Times, 21
wealth gap
  contributes to police misconduct and
    racism, 61–62
Weaver, Randy, 21, 156

Wilbur, John, 42
Wilson, James Q., 73
Wilson, Lynne, 124
Wilson, Michael F., 65, 69

zero tolerance strategy, 49–51, 111
  has increased police misconduct cases,
    65–66
  reexamination of, 108
  see also assertive/aggressive policing